EDGAR LEE MASTERS

Edgar Lee Masters as a young man

EDGAR LEE MASTERS

*A Biographical Sketchbook
about a Famous American Author*

Hardin Wallace Masters

Rutherford • Madison • Teaneck
Fairleigh Dickinson University Press
London: Associated University Presses

Also by HARDIN WALLACE MASTERS:
Edgar Lee Masters: A Centenary Memoir-Anthology

7/1978
Am. Let.

Associated University Presses, Inc.
Cranbury, New Jersey 08512

PS
3525
A83
Z77

Associated University Presses
Magdalen House
136–148 Tooley Street
London SE1 2TT, England

Library of Congress Cataloguing in Publication Data

Masters, Hardin Wallace, 1899–
   Edgar Lee Masters.

   Bibliography: p.
   Includes index.
   1. Masters, Edgar Lee, 1869–1950—Biography.
2. Authors, American—20th century—Biography.
PS3525.A83Z77   811'.5'2[B]   76-29337
ISBN 0-8386-2031-0

The author wishes to thank the Thomas Y. Crowell Company,
Inc., for permission to quote from *"Herndon's Life of Lincoln"*
with a Newly Revised Introduction by Paul M. Angle by William
H. Herndon and Jesse W. Weik.

*To the memory of the people of Spoon River
in the State of Illinois and especially my forebears:*

Edgar Lee Masters
Hardin Wallace Masters
Squire Davis Masters

Contents

7

List of Illustrations

Foreword

Poets, like opera singers, age early, so that forty-five is quite an old age for a poet. But that was exactly the age when Edgar Lee Masters burst upon the American reading public with *Spoon River Anthology,* which catapulted him into national fame and immediately won for him a permanent place in the history of American literature. He had written five volumes of poetry before the historic date of 1915, and afterward he wrote more than three dozen other books of verse, essays, fiction, and biography, but it is *Spoon River Anthology,* chiefly, that will keep his name secure in our literary annals. It has gone into about 100 editions in hard cover and paperback, and it has been translated into several languages including Arabic, Chinese, Korean, and Czech. It has been dramatized more than once, and an opera titled *La Collina* ("The Hill", a central poem in the anthology), written by Mario Pergallo, was performed at La Scala.

Masters originally conceived *Spoon River Anthology* as a novel, a fatalistic narrative with strong elements of social criticism, for Masters was a liberal-progressive in the heady sense of the Theodore Roosevelt-Senator Robert La Follette philosophies. Indeed, he was one of the earliest Angry Men in American Poetry, as May Swenson felicitously calls him. Along with Carl Sandburg and Vachel Lindsay he was one of the major heralds of a new dawn in American poetry. These three did nothing less, after Walt Whitman, of course, than democratize American poetry. Not that they did not react to the song in nature and the delights of love. They were more startled by the varied plights of the silent majority of misery that the Industrial Revolution plus the machinations of the Robber Barons had inflicted upon the nation. The three turned their observations into verses both ringing and lyrical.

Masters was probably, technically speaking, the most original of the three. In his glorious monologues, an era in American history spoke with both sorrowful recollection and philosophical resignation from the grave, which to Masters became one huge confessional. Chase Henry and Daisy Fraser and Deacon Thomas Rhodes, and the 241 others in the *Anthology* are the witnesses of the America of their day, and also of the general human condition at all times and places.

The form of the individual poems was so novel that some academic and other critics denounced the *Anthology* outright as being neither prose nor poetry, while more perceptive commentators admitted the power of the poems but at the same time expressed bewilderment at Masters's technique. Of course, Masters, genuine artist that he was, created his own technique, and the general reading public, which bought his book in the tens of thousands, showed better judgment than the academicians and professional critics. Are all the poems in the *Anthology* of equal excellence? Of course not. Only second-rate artists are always at their best. There are still fanatical formalists, like the late Alfred Kreymborg, who insist that the *Anthology* "contributed little to American poetry, a great deal to American prose." This view is rapidly vanishing. The more generally accepted view is well expressed by May Swenson, a fine poet herself: "In *Spoon River,* Masters borrowed the mouths of the dead to give outlet to all his grudges, beliefs, indignations, insights, prophesies, discoveries of glaring injustice, revelations of life's mysteries and paradoxes. . . . Miraculously he

12

also created and bequeathed to us a world in microcosm, new in form, timeless in essence."

What sort of man performed this miracle? From one point of view, the most unlikely of men. He had spent only one year at Knox College, was largely self-taught, "read law" in his father's office, and became a prosperous lawyer in Chicago. Always he wanted to be a writer, but for years he imitated the classic English poets—Keats, Shelley, Swinburne, Milton. What appeared to be most urgent in his personality was the desire to express his outrage at the gross social injustices about him. He thus oscillated between imitation and indignation. Then, largely through the most understanding guidance of William Marion Reedy, editor of a magazine in St. Louis, *Reedy's Mirror*—one of the great, still not fully appreciated editors in American periodical literature—Masters found himself and earned an enduring place in American literature.

But what kind of father was Masters? Husband? Lawyer? What was his attitude toward women? Precisely what were his politics? Did he have any religious impulse? How much of a family man was he? How did he get along with Clarence Darrow, his law partner for eight years, 1903-1911? Who were his favorite authors? What women inspired him? No one knew him better in these respects than his son, Hardin W. Masters, author of the present volume. He is a business man, civic leader, banker. He makes no pretensions to being a critic of poetry—"I like it or I don't like it, but I never know why." But he was deeply attached to his father, listened to him across the years, and clearly his affection and devotion were returned. His present book is, obviously, not written in any traditional mode of criticism or biography. Rather, it is a series of brief sketches of his father *en pantouffles,* as the French would say. Here he is in the bosom of his family, in his law office, in the company of men and women who stimulated him. Here he

13

is "unbuttoned", discussing serious issues and engaging in small talk. His son's sketches of him in all these aspects are candid camera shots, so to speak, that add up to a revealing portrait of a great poet. Nobody else could have written this sort of book. It is an important contribution to the understanding of the poet and of his time. It will undoubtedly offer insights to all future literary critics and historians.

Charles Angoff

Preface

Edgar Lee Masters was my pal, my friend and counselor, for a period of twenty years, not limited to this period of time but, tuned in to my life in an emphatic way. In recounting some of our times together in Chicago, New York, Spring Lake, Michigan, and other places, people ask me why I did not write a book about them. Some people even go so far as to tell me that I am a lazy son—neglecting my heritage and obligations. So it is that over the past eight years I have developed the following sketches as the subject matter forced me to the typewriter, and as time permitted.

The book is described as a *sketchbook* because it is different in major respects from the biographies I've read; it has the unique advantage of the short story supported by the factual incentive of my own personal memories. It is a series of sketches—so vivid to me as to be just that. I must add that since I was ten years old I have believed that my father would attain immortality by the efforts of his writing. Thus the belief commanded action, and I have collected and maintained a store of available information—letters, pictures, diaries, and memoranda beyond my abilities of evaluation during most of that time.

Consequently, this book is addressed, in a general way, not only to the biography addicts but more particularly to the lovers of American poetry, as well as to the collectors of Masters. It is written from the heart. First the heart of a boy, then the heartless judgment of a high school youth; later, it is written with the know-it-all attitude of the young man of twenty to his early thirties. Finally, now as a biased reviewer of his family scene, and today when time becomes so important to my own life span, I feel that it is a contribution to the story of Edgar Lee Masters that some day will be written by a competent and analytical biographer. As such I hope this book will be used accordingly. I hope that it will reveal some facets of my father's life, a life that sometimes seems to the readers of *Spoon River Anthology* to have been something that it never was. With this thought, here it is; and welcome to my reservoir of memories. Edgar Lee Masters died twenty-five years ago. His books live on.

Ghost Ranch, New Mexico

H.W.M.

Introduction

It seems to me that even a casual friend of Edgar Lee Masters, the Man from Spoon River, would have observed that three things in his life were of prime importance. The most obvious of these motivating concerns was his fascination with books. This lifelong companionship with the thoughts of others, as expressed by his favorite authors, was apparent to even a remote friend or guest in our home.

However, the most basic and important thing to him and to the world portrayed by his pen was woman. He spent much of his emotional life trying to understand them, not to say worship them, but never succeeded. This might be amended to say that, when he did succeed, it was too late to be of significance in his life.

The third characteristic interest that stands out in my recollection was his aloofness or indifference to most people. It seemed at times to be timidity. To say that he was an introvert only partially describes this "going it alone" attitude of his. So the three interests in the order of importance to him as an individual are women, books and aloneness.

There was not a period of his life, under my mature observation, from Chicago to New York, that was not under the influence of a woman. This does not mean that he was in love or emotionally involved during this time. It means that he was influenced by a woman in some phase of his daily life—in writing, reading, traveling, or spiritual reactions. These periods of involvement were indicated not by what he said but by his silences. Like every man's life, some

17

of his ladies were inspirational and good, others were malevolent and bad; however, all of them became slides for his microscopic analysis of the irony, pathos, or humor of the incident, as he happened to classify it. He turned from poet to cynic in due course; it was just a matter of time. It is not difficult for me to go through his *Selected Poems* and relate the poem to the woman. Each woman must be imagined and stressed by those readers of his poetry in the interest of a more complete understanding of his works.

EDGAR LEE MASTERS

Beginning

Rain was dripping on the red tin roof, and the window framed a forlorn backyard. A soot-blackened oak tree swayed in the early winter winds, and the gray sky promised snow.

A somber-looking man in his early forties gazed out the window at this familiar scene and occasionally tapped his heavy writing pencil on the surface of a small mission table. The room was austere and the furnishing heavy. Reluctantly, the man's eyes returned to a pad of white paper and the pencil returned to the growing string of words. His thoughts returned from the top of the black oak to the Mason County Hills of his youth. He smiled sardonically at the small backyard and decided the name of his next poem would be "Hod Putt."

The man was a Chicago lawyer named Lee Masters. The small back bedroom of his house had been his hideaway since the free verse poems had absorbed his home life away from his "Loop" law office.

The sound of the delivery boy coming through the areaway with groceries again distracted his thoughts and he removed his steel-rimmed glasses and rubbed his eyes. He thought of his father in Springfield, Illinois. He could see him pacing with his light shotgun for a quail hunt with his old crony John Armstrong—it was that time. He could not get back to work this day, and so he let his thoughts drift back over the years as dusk crept into the room and the black oak tree swayed in the freshening wind off Lake Michigan.

His mother, Emma Jerusha Masters, née Dexter, had told him that he was born in Garnett, Kansas, just after the Civil War. Fortunately he had no memories of the brief months in this small town, one of his father's adjustments to the economic pattern that seemed to follow his entire life. His mother spoke infrequently of his birth but did tell him that it was on a stifling day, August 23, 1869, and that he was the first of four children, all born in stifling weather, all gifted, brilliant, and destined for better days.

The birthplace of Edgar Lee Masters, Garnett, Kansas. Original sketch by M. J. Grace.

Law Office—Petersburg, Illinois

The familiar, worn, wooden stair creaked as Lee Masters ran up to his father's law office. There was the hot silence of a central Illinois noonday and he was getting out to see his pony. First was this errand that took him by the office; the smell of worn leather and tobacco; the silence of a vacant space, usually occupied by a hearty man.

He put his package on the table in Hardy Masters's office and looked over the Petersburg square. On one corner was Judge Bent's office, and across the way the drugstore where he had seen Dorothy Painter watching him out of the corner of her dark eyes. His mother said that if his father took "better care" of his law business he could go to Knox Academy at Galesburg and study Latin under a fine man from the East. He thought of his pony out at the farm, and it seemed that his father might have the same feeling for his horses and his hunting. Did he really want to go to Knox this much? Life was long, practically without end for him, whereas his father was getting old. Well, he wasn't going to beg any more or talk about it. He would take his father's part for a change and keep a stoical silence when the subject of neglecting his law practice came up. Also, he realized, it wouldn't be too long until he might have a law practice of his own to worry about. He would have to study his law right here in this small office overlooking the square, and probably it would be just as hot and he had better start taking a man's viewpoint.

Father rushed down the stairs to the street and looked

around the square for his grandfather's buckboard. He was to ride out to the farm for a visit. Glorious days were ahead for him. His grandparents were the finest people in the world, he was sure. Many times he felt guilty when it came over him that he "got along better" at the farm than he did at home. He kicked at the hitching post in his impatience to get going. Still, no buckboard came. He hoped Lucinda had baked those wondrous "graham gems" and perhaps some sugar cookies. Uncle Wilbur Masters was to have a can of fresh worms ready for fishing in the morning—but the best of all was his own pony, named Beauty, which grandfather had given him. Beauty would be waiting to go, and he would again dream of racing Indians and saving Dorothy from a fate worse than death by riding double out of the danger area.

He saw Squire Davis's distinguished face across the way and he would help out with the shopping. He dashed away.

This was ELM's story as we walked the square in Petersburg, Illinois.

Spring Lake, Michigan

One lovely June morning, I heard Father singing in his room: "H-A-R-R-I-G-A-N spells Harrigan. Proud of all the Irish blood that's in me—never a man can say a word agin me. H-A-R-R-I-G-A-N you see—Is a name that the shame never has been connected with—Harrigan, that's me." I can hear him to this day, singing and chuckling over this absurd song. It amused him greatly and his rendition of it while shaving always meant a good-spirited day ahead.

Shortly, I heard the bedroom door open. This was the signal for me to run down from my room on the third floor and see what might be going on. He said to me, "My boy, I believe we will go over to the farm tonight, if I can get a cabin on the boat."

The farm was our beloved place at Spring Lake, Michigan. It was a retreat that Father never got tired of and was the cradle of many poems and much farm work. Later it became a refuge for him in his travail.

The road from our Spring Lake house to the main road was a mile or more of sandy loam; it wound through the blackberry patch, a small orchard, and around a copse of lovely trees. The trees were the nightly meeting place of our crows. I guess every farm has its crow family, and we had them, much to my father's delight. He thought them to be wise, noisy, and silly, but loved to hear them talking—cawing as they flew around the farm. He would stop, remove his sweat-stained old hat, listen to them talk, and smile to himself as if he knew what they were talking about. I would identify the crow as the bird on his coat of arms, his bird. I must add that the crow and the robin evoked a strange counterpart in his poetic soul. Father told me one day that each spring brought him closer to the winter. The crow was a mysterious bird—a bird of ill omen for him. It was such a strange comparison that his comment has stayed with me for over fifty years; I never see the black crow that it does not evoke the image of my father—standing in the road, hoe in his hand, hat on the back of his head, and looking to the sky where the crows were flying home to roost.

He loved the bird, its color, its intelligence, but, above all, he loved the recollection of its call across the meadows and streams of Central Illinois. I have seen him stop a hundred times to listen to the crows and he would always say just that: "Listen to the crows, my boy." It was wrung from the innermost being, a terribly solemn cry that spelled a great loneliness for him, I am sure.

Nostalgic days on our beloved Michigan farm.

Lake Boat

The night was windless. Black water to the stern of the S.S. *Manitou* reflected the lights from the Wrigley Building. To the north came the hum of traffic along the Lake Shore Drive. The year was 1912.

A middle-aged man, puffing a pipe, stood by the rail of the steamship and looked out past the crib and the breakwater. The man was my father, and I felt that he was trying to race the clock ahead to dawn. Then would come the gray water of the other side and the dunes of the Michigan shore. Then the boat would be gliding into the harbor at Grand Haven, Michigan, and the noises of landing would mingle with the familiar sounds of the Grand River marshes.

Crossing Lake Michigan was a never-ending source of wonder and happiness to the poet. He had analyzed the boat sounds, the moods of the lake, the people of the boat in the same manner he wrote a law brief or cross-examined a witness. He knew this water, beginning at the Rush Street Bridge and ending with the eastern shores, intimately. All that was in him compelled him to take a lake boat trip. I believe it was one of the reasons for his purchase and deep attachment to our Spring Lake farm—you could take the boat and get there.

I always enjoyed these junkets, usually taken on Friday night and returning on Sunday night. We sometimes talked late into the night on the leeside of the boat, stretched out in deck chairs. Here was talk at its best for my father—

27

night, starlight, mystical splash of prow water, and the darkness stretching away into eternity. Here, as a young man in high school, I propounded the age-old questions: love, marriage, children, God, old age, friends and enemies, the gamut of the mind. And let me say that my father was not an atheist as some have said. He was a man who worshipped the world of our Lord and all that was in it. He often told me of the deep faith of his grandfather, Squire Davis Masters, and how much his Christian principles contributed to the happiness of his life and to the summers he, my father, had spent on the Masters's farm north of Petersburg. He loved and revered his grandmother for holding the same basic love of our Lord and for the peace and love she brought others as a result of her religion.

I said one time: "Father, you are getting along, how does it feel?" His reply was, "My boy, until the very last, you never notice growing older. It is such a gradual process and so well masked." His life was that way until the last few years. He was living each day in its own special concept. He never noticed growing old until the very last. And at the end, I stood in the Harrison Street Station and watched the modest casket switched to the train for the last ride to Springfield and Petersburg, Illinois.

My Dear Girl

In my grandfather's law office, 308 Reisch Building, Springfield, Illinois, was a large, handsome mahogany desk that belonged to one of his young partners, Walter T. Day. The desk has now been refinished and moved to the Masters Memorial Home in Petersburg, Illinois, thanks to the thoughtfulness of his widow, Mrs. Walter Day. In a hidden compartment of the desk the following letter was found:

Lower Alton, January 30th 1834

Dear Miss,
I with pleasure improve the present opportunity to inform you that I received your present with many thanks to you for such an expression of kindness—I read the contents of yours—with a degree of pleasure unknown to my heart. My Dear Girl if what you say in your kind present be the language of your heart, it is the most excellent and dearest gift to my heart I ever received. I was glad to hear you mention one thing which was that you did not wish to trifle with any pensive feelings. It is a fact which I hope you will keep in mind. Think not Miss that I flatter you for I say it free from flattery. That your many accomplishments and agreeable manners have gained that seat in my mind and affections which will ever entitle you to my kindest treatment and tenderest friendship. These are facts which I would gladly have

29

made known to you before but could not dare to hope for the least return from you. I speak not from the impulse of the present moment but I speak of a matter well considered and permit me to speak free and tell that in you centered all my hope of future happiness—for my dear friend you possess all the charms and qualifications necessary to render me perfectly happy—in married life —excuse me if you perhaps think I am intruding upon your time and patience and perhaps I am venturing too far without hearing from you again but if I have said or done anything amiss I beg you to excuse me. And at any rate let me have an answer to this which I shall look for with anxiety. You will find this in a work pocket designed as a present. In the same you may find a few kisses as a token of the unchanging love I have for you after writing a verse more. I will conclude for I fear I have trespassed too long upon your time already.

The heart that dictates is thine, the hand that writes shall be if my offer you should find a prize worth accepting. If this I win let me hear your answer soon. I remain dear Miss—yours forever.

S. D. Masters

Miss Lucinda Wasson
P.S. Please pardon the mistakes if you find any for I have not looked over.

The simplicity and dignity of the letter speak out, particularly in the decade of the 70s. It is quoted because of my father's adoration of his grandfather, Squire Davis Masters. It bespeaks some of the characteristics of ELM's moods and heritage in a way nothing else could possibly do. I am grateful to Samuel S. Blane of Petersburg, Illinois, for sending me a copy for the sketchbook.

Prairie Breeze

The old Squire Davis Masters farm lies about six miles north of Petersburg, Illinois. It is beautiful country, rather typical of the lush State of Illinois. I had the opportunity of seeing the old barn before it burned down, and before this had a visit with my great grandmother, Lucinda, before she died. This was about 1909, and my father took great pride in arranging this trip. I wish I had been older and had received more of an impression of the place and the pioneers who settled it.

However, I do remember that Lucinda was bedridden in a lovely, sunny room in the farm residence. The prairie breeze gently lifted the white curtains in the room, and my father sat in a little rocking chair, lost in his memories of boyhood days. I tried to talk with Lucinda but found it difficult. I was not familiar with the silences of strong and independent people, nor had I ever known such a beautiful face, nor had I ever seen such faith and repose as shone from her face. Father would come to, periodically, and fiix Lucinda with his well-known and inscrutable gaze. I knew that he was saying, "I may never see her again." So he rocked and dreamed. The wind from the farm of his childhood stirred the curtain, and Lucinda's thin, lovely hands stroked the coverlet of her bed. I felt that I was a stranger and should leave. I was young and uninhibited, so I did.

I went outside and talked to a strange farmhand. He was unaware of my background or the sentiment of the place.

I got little out of him, but tried to place the various incidents of Father's life on the farm, as they related to the buildings. I could see my great-grandfather carrying slop to the hogs. I could visualize the story about Abe Lincoln's trying a law case out under the maple trees, and I could hear the voices from Lucinda's bedroom murmuring about the inevitable flight of time that had taken place since his youth on this beloved place. I felt great emotions in the air and a stir of things in the sunlight that I could not understand.

ELM, in turn, was having his tribulations with his grandmother who understood him so well and loved him so much. She was saying goodbye to him and giving him counsel that he might not accept and, maybe, never understood.

My Mother

My mother had golden hair and was a very lovely lady. She was frugal and possessed a fine sense of values. Her ability to hunt "bargains," which she stored in a large closet, was a family joke that ever seemed to cause great amusement. However, during my sixth-grade days, she found a

Father lived in this Georgian brick house, 4853 Kenwood Avenue, Chicago, from 1909 until he moved to New York City in 1925. Mother lived here with my sister Marcia until 1942 or thereabouts. Much of Spoon River Anthology *was written here.*

33

house that she proceeded to sell my father on. It proved to be an attractive value, and we moved to 4853 Kenwood Avenue on the South Side of Chicago. I believe the next decade proved to be my father's happiest and most productive years in many ways.

The bedroom on the second floor of our house on Kenwood Avenue had two large windows that faced the west. It was a bright, comfortable room with a large colonial, four-poster bed. On the mantel over the fireplace, Father's old clock ticked away in solemn rhythm. The clock was named Tursey Potter and was an original Seth Thomas clock from Plymouth Hollow, Connecticut. Tursey Potter stood on the mantel and softly ticked away many couplets and meters. The clock had belonged to father's grandfather, Squire Davis Masters, and was a most treasured heirloom. The door of the clock was embellished with a bee hive on which were the words, "By industry we thrive." This out-of-fashion phrase, however, set the tempo of father's bedroom, for it was to be his workshop. Here in his spare time, on weekends and some evenings, he toiled away with his works. The room had a fireplace and a dormer window and exuded an air of light and quietude. When Father was working in this room, the door was closed and my mother tiptoed about the house and demanded that I play outside. Silence was the order of the day.

Many's the time on my way to the third floor and my quarters, I passed his room as quietly as youthful spirits permitted. The image of his bent head over a pad of paper, looking up every little while to the sunset, is one of the zinc-clear etchings in my mental gallery of him. I cannot think of the room and his hand flowing over his pad of writing paper without smelling his gorgeous pipes. He seldom cleaned these briars, but loved them with the passion of a studious man. He smoked one of the trade-name blends, and the room comes to me in pipe odor and pencil shavings and the soft hiss of his soft-leaded pencils. Parts of *Spoon River* were born in this room over a period of many months.

Here in this same room came many visitors—I remember the night Carl Sandburg came and talked through to the late hours. It was also a favorite visiting place of my grandfather, Hardin Wallace Masters, who decried the time father spent away from his law books, but entered into the spirit of the room nonetheless.

Other prominent people came to the house. The large living room, downstairs, on Kenwood Avenue, was impressive. It might have been in an English manor, perhaps Stratford-on-Avon; it was long and dark, oak bookcases ran the entire length of the south wall, a large fireplace sputtered comfortably between them. Common to the spaciousness of the times, the room had a high ceiling and excellent acoustics.

Jack Powys, Theodore Dreiser, and Vachel Lindsay had voices that cannot be forgotten and that crept up the stairway on sonorous knees to my waiting ears. I was supposed to be sound asleep but found myself sitting on the top stair with both ears attuned to catch some remark for posterity or, better yet, the bawdy story.

Mother was an accomplished musician and Father often ended the "visiting" with a request that she play "Clare de Lune" or another of his favorite pieces on her piano.

Playing Marbles

At the address 4406 Greenwood Avenue, on the South Side of Chicago, was a four-story, red-brick apartment building, facing east, and with a wonderful south exposure. We lived on the top floor and received the full benefit of the sun and air. The neighbors with whom ELM seemed to have the most contact were the Deans, next door to the south, and the Bithers, to the north.

At this time, I was attending the Shakespeare School on the corner of 46th and Greenwood. Across the street was the Kenwood Evangelical Church, not an inspiration to ELM. He disliked the minister and, as a result, attended infrequently.

One vivid recollection of this time was my passion for playing marbles in the school yard. Father, in turn, often related his fondness for the game and bought me a very fine cornelian shooter. I remember my adoration of the man when he came home one night with this gift. He sat on the living room rug with me and fired away with his gift until I became very concerned about getting it for myself. It was on occasions of this kind that he reminisced about his boyhood. He loved to relive his Petersburg days even at that time, and often commented on what I was missing as a city boy.

A favorite story of his youth concerned the summers he spent with his grandparents on the Masters farm, The Maples, north of Petersburg. He worshipped both of them, even to the point of favoring his grandmother over everyone else. What does a man with the capacity of painting Spoon River in eternal colors think of as a boy? What fancies crossed his mind while he lay in the sun of the Menard County Hills? He told me of his summers on the farm, of his daydreaming in the sun, many times lying on his back in the long grass and watching the summer clouds race across the horizon for hours at a time. Was *Domesday Book* born in the grasses? I have always believed that the beneficent influence of Squire Davis and Lucinda Masters played a major part in the good side of my father. I say good side because, like all of us, he had a bad side as well— a bitter, cynical, sarcastic side to his character that was devastating in a court room or on a sheet of paper. A brush dipped in burning acid—once smeared with this brush, you avoided another coat.

Summer Job

Father said to me, "We are going to the Central Trust Company to see my friend, Charlie Dawes." As we walked down Monroe Street together from the Illinois Central Station on Michigan Avenue, he related the fact that he and Charles Gates Dawes had been friends for some years. It had been an instinctive and rewarding friendship. Father told me of his admiration for Dawes—of his courage, his high ideals and business standards, but that Dawes was a conservative man.

We arrived at the bank and went into Dawes's office. It was comfortable and efficiently arranged. He told him that I was a sophomore in high school and needed a summer job, not only to pay my way in school, but to keep me from wasting my time.

Dawes fixed me with what is known as a banker's cold eye and asked me what I could do. I told him nothing much except I was interested in manual training and building wireless sets.

He and my father laughed heartily at this candid answer and proceeded to ignore me. They went into a lengthy business and political discussion and finally ended up with a story about Grover Cleveland. I listened intently and wondered why it took so long to get a job. All this time ELM was relaxed in a comfortable chair, twisting his watch chain, a frequent mannerism of his when visiting, nodding his head, and laughing at some of Charlie Dawes's cryptic remarks.

Finally he returned to our mission. "Well, Charlie, he's

a good boy and needs a job badly. I hoped he could work here in the bank." Dawes picked up his phone and said, "Better yet, I'll get him a spot with Henry, my brother." He did. Henry Dawes was a wonderful man, he had a fine office; where I became office boy until school started.

We left the bank. Father dismissed me with the remark that I'd better start home and rest up for my new work, if I got the job. He added that this was probably as close as any Masters would ever get to being a banker. I know now that this was indeed a facetious remark. He sometimes sang a song about a banker that went something like this: "Goes to church on Sunday and passes the contribution box. Tall silk hat and white cravat. He's just as cunning as a fox. . . ."

In my library are two volumes entitled *A Journal of the Great Wars* by Charles G. Dawes, inscribed, "For Edgar Lee Masters with Best Regards from Charles G. Dawes, dated July 30, 1922."

I have always remembered this event rather vividly because it was typical of Father's broad and diverse contacts. His appeal as a man to many different people, from Dreiser to Dawes, would be a fair example of this range of friendships. An interesting contrast in friends.

Fun Place

At Tabors, the St. Joe River flows by like a majestic brown ribbon being shaken in the sun. My recollection of this, one of many favorite Michigan vacation spots, goes way back—but I'm afraid it's mostly hearsay. However, the place played a part in the recreation of the man of this book.

It was a fun place for Father—modest and interesting for awhile, because it was away from the law office and out of the heat of the city. I have been told that he enjoyed fishing and spent much time at it. This does not jibe with my recollection or experience, but that's characteristic of fish stories. He talked a good trip and many times expressed the wish to go and get a good bass, but it was not a recreation or a sport that enthralled him. It seems to me that he used the water, with a pole in his hand, as a background for writing. His crayon and mental slate ran best when he was dreaming and relaxed. He told me many times that word images or pictures came to him readily while watching a bobber or casting a line. But more importantly, he stored this material with great fidelity for transcription to his workpad at a later time.

Well, Tabors set a good table, as the saying goes. The cabins were attractive and it was a place for visiting. One summer my grandfather, called either Hardy or H. W. as suited my grandmother's mood at the moment, was with us for a fine visit; and later on, Bill Reedy, who played such an important part in Father's creative life, came to visit. Reedy was the editor of *Reedy's Mirror,* a publication that was as familiar in the Masterses' house as the Sears catalogue. He was a man of vast reading and an astute judge of good writers. He had a faculty for picking them out before fame came their way. He was a fat, hearty Rabelaisian character, beloved of all of us and devoted to my father. If I had to pick the individual or circumstance that was basic to the development of Father's writing and the birth of Spoon River, I would name William Marion Reedy of St. Louis, Missouri, as the individual who blew Father off the starting mat.

It was places like Tabors, where they were together for a few days of talk and nonsense, that were milestones in Father's literary road.

I remember their sitting in the sun on the banks of the St. Joe, talking endlessly. My mother would join the "grown-ups" for awhile, but ultimately she tired of the books, books, and more books that dominated their interest, and moved off to other pursuits. In the meantime, I had dug the worms, carried the poles to the boat, and wanted some action. Finally they would move leisurely to the boat, bringing some books along. Father often rowed and was cautioned by Bill to take it easy because he was a floater, not a swimmer. "Right over there, Lee, under yon willow lies a bass." Many times Bill was right about fish, as well as about books and the men who wrote them. I found the letter written to me by Reedy, when I went off to World War I with my head in the clouds. Here it is:

William Marion Reedy
St. Louis

June 21, 1918

So you are off to the war! I congratulate and envy you. You are putting your hand to and your heart and life in

41

the greatest work now in the world to do—the finest thing to do since man boggled God's fair creation. Here's an elderly codger's God speed to you. The work may be often, as Masefield says, "damned dull, damned dirty and damned dangerous" but the spirit you take into it will disinfect it of all that. Keep hand and heart and body clean as you follow duty. You are "on the job" of broadening freedom in the world—and freedom is the cure for all the evils of the earth. Remember that what you are out to kill is the power of one set of men to ride on the backs of other men. Don't do anything you'd not want father, mother, Marcia, Madeline to know. Deliver the goods when called upon to do so. Fear nothing but being untrue to yourself and your blood. Love the things true and beautiful that outlast death. And write now and then to Old Bill. Affectionately

William Marion Reedy

It might be stressed that the writer of this inspiring letter was, in fact, the godfather of *Spoon River Anthology*. It is quoted here not because it is written to the author of this sketchbook but because it was important to Edgar Lee Masters, the creator of *Spoon River Anthology*. The letter reflects so accurately Bill Reedy's interest in people and causes. It also reflects and radiates the reason Reedy and Masters were such devoted friends. The fine motivation of Reedy in ELM's life, and his lifelong gratitude, become readily apparent. I cannot overemphasize Bill Reedy's influence in his literary vision and way of life.

Walking-Talking

A man's life can be judged by examining his different activities. One of Edgar Lee Masters's outstanding interests was light exercise. He loved to go walking and walked regularly and at some distance. To this he added the companionship of many interesting people. Walking in the outdoors, he examined books, philosophies, art, and a myriad of subjects through the eyes of friends.

For a period of some ten years of his life he walked every Sunday, he being a vigorous man of forty-eight planning walking trips in advance, much as he planned his reading, writing, and other recreational activities. At this time I was in high school and did not always enjoy having my Sundays taken up in this manner, but Father was the boss and I went along. Many thanks to his memory now.

Older companions varied with the years as friends dropped along the way. Among the first and most glamorous walkers was Judge Kenesaw Mountain Landis. The picture of these two, swinging through Jackson Park in Chicago, comes back with no effort to my memory tubes. They were a distinguished looking pair often fierce of countenance, talking avidly, and swinging good substantial sticks as they walked hundreds of miles together. Another occasional companion was Abraham Meyer of Chicago's famous Mayer, Meyer, Austrian & Platt firm. Another was Samuel M. Morgan, whom my father befriended in the desolation of his divorce. Morgan lived at our home for several years and was a man of fine and cultured habits.

He was the perfect introvert and did not have time for most people. Father met him in the course of his law practice and, as Morgan was a court reporter, sent him business. This legal contact soon blossomed into a fine friendship, and Sam Morgan apparently thrived under Father's caustic wit and mental gymnastics. As a matter of fact, Morgan inspired him to ribaldry, monkey shines, and foolishness. They discussed without end books and many other things that made little sense to their young, high school walking companion.

Short walks in the city grew into long days in the country. One of our favorite spots became the Indiana dunes. The three of us would leave the city on an early train on Sunday and go to Tremont. This little station on the South Shore Electric became the hub of wonderful walks in the dune country. What memories and what walks! Suffice to say, we would return late and weary; walking the average three miles an hour, we must have covered fifteen miles on many days. This went on the year round except during the zero weather of the winter months.

This type of weekend paid big dividends in father's health. He was ever a healthy and robust individual, but at the same time worked long hours. In addition to his law practice, and a good one it was, contrary to some commentators, he was recovering from the birth of *Spoon River Anthology*. This book had proved a terrific drain on his stamina, particularly so because he was already mentally writing its successor, *The Great Valley*. I remember his writing part of a poem, called "Slip Shoe Lovey," on the back of an envelope and reading it to me with some glee.

On these Sundays we often discussed the education that he had been denied. He insisted that I work hard and develop the ability to concentrate and be scholarly in my ways. He recounted many times his difficulties in getting the kind of book and literary nourishment that he needed

44

as a growing boy. Much of his knowledge, not to say erudition, came from his own grubbing over the years. One phase typical of this was his pursuit of law and passing the bar examination. He told me of his work in his father's law office, of the arduous manner in which he became one of the Chicago Bar Association's most distinguished members. In my eyes at the time, he was in many ways a better lawyer than a poet. Nevertheless, to understand the man, I believe you must feel that his writing supplemented his legal ability, and vice versa.

Although Father wrote substantially more prose than poetry, *Spoon River Anthology* eclipsed all of his other books.

No Club Man

ELM, all his life long, was a vigorous man. No illness to speak of for many years, he trained himself like a Spartan and believed in cold baths every morning. He watched his diet and participated faithfully in exercise of various kinds, walking, gardening, and swimming being his favorites. So it was over the years that he went along in health and well-being. Like most of us, finally he was his own worst enemy. He worried about finances and became contemptuous of some friends. His bachelor years invited strange diets that did him no good. This combination finally brought the great reader, the tolerant philosopher, and the cynic, to his death bed in Melrose Park, Pennsylvania.

I think of the many Saturdays I met father at the Illinois Athletic Club in Chicago for a swim. This was a treat for me, and apparently he enjoyed telling all hands in the Bath Department that I was his boy. I was scrawny, a mediocre swimmer, but to his black friends, the bath attendants, I was the coming world's champion of something. We would steam, swim, rub, and then sit beside the pool and have lunch. For many years of his life he was a swimmer in this pool. When he moved to New York, he continued his swimming at the YMCA near the Chelsea Hotel. We believed that it was one reason for his many years of superb health.

The Illinois Athletic Club picture has been in my mind for portrayal and interpretation. It is most vivid and represents a side of my father not too well known. He was not

46

the club-man type, but he loved the IAC as he loved all things that were a phase of good living. He liked good food. He liked to be waited on. He liked the adoration of his club servants. He always had a special greeting for the blacks and they loved him. He was, in fact, a teller of Negro stories in the steam room, on the train, getting a shoe shine, or any place where he had a special friend. They all acknowledged this technique and acted as willing conspirators to his foolishness, which usually started with a most dignified greeting, such as, "Good morning, Edward, I trust you're well," or, "Kind regards to you, Morton, and I hope you haven't been indulging in liquor." This touched off much merriment, and the act went on in all seriousness, much to everyone's enjoyment.

Special names or nicknames were a specialty of his; he could create one on the spur of the moment, and usually they fitted the individual like a good Western boot. He used them both with joy and with a devilish leer in his eye, if they were particularly descriptive, but they were seldom malicious. Likewise, he would tell stories about himself and others in a most deflating manner. I remember his story about his brother Tom, in which he said that Tom always stayed at the Great Northern Hotel in Chicago. I asked him why that particular hotel? His reply was that his brother liked anything with "great" in it. You see, not malicious, but a head-on-the-side remark. Another fine thrust was at Frank Walker, a Chicago attorney, who told father that his library contained twice the number of books that Father's did. ELM replied, "I know it, Frank, but the trouble is, you haven't read them."

47

Rough Rider

My father was a great admirer of Theodore Roosevelt. They had what the French call rapport, perhaps stimulated by the friendship of Teddy's sister, Mrs. Corrine Roosevelt Robinson. In any event, the two men corresponded and visited back and forth whenever possible.

So it came to be that in the early part of 1917, my father was invited to Oyster Bay for a visit with Teddy Roosevelt. He left Chicago in high spirits and it was evident to all of us that he anticipated with joy the impending visit. He said to me before departing, "My boy, is there something I can bring you from New York?" I said, "Father, I think Teddy Roosevelt is a terrifiic guy. If you would have him autograph a piece of paper for me, I'd certainly treasure it." Father said, "I'll do it."

It turned out to be a great visit between two men, both perhaps rough riders; one mentally, the other physically. My father said that Oyster Bay was just the place for such a visit.

In my library is the book entitled *The Strenuous Life* by Theodore Roosevelt. It is inscribed as follows: "To Hardin Wallace Masters: 'Don't flinch; don't foul; hit the line hard!' Theodore Roosevelt, Feb. 1st 1917." This was the autographed piece of paper brought back by Father. He reported that when he said, "I have a boy who is a great admirer of yours, Teddy, and if you would autograph a card for him, he would be ever so happy," Roosevelt is reported to have replied, "Hell, Lee, I'll do better than that. Your boy should read *The Strenuous Life* and I'll fix it for him right now."

President Roosevelt's talented sister, Corrine, who was fond of my father, had published a book of poems through Charles Scribner's Sons about 1921. ELM thought it a good book; it was topically arranged with parts on life, love, heroism, grief, service, and sacrifice. The copy he gave me years ago as a keepsake is inscribed as follows: "For my friend Edgar Lee Masters, whose poem on my beloved brother Theodore Roosevelt gives a new picture of him at his home Sagamore Hill, such as has been given by no one else. For that poem and for many others I am his grateful admirer." The first time I read this treasured volume I was startled—in the back of the book is a lock of brown hair. It is there today.

Percy Grainger

The old house on the South Side of Chicago holds some of my most poignant memories of Father. It seems but a few years ago that I sat unnoticed on the stairway from the first to the second floors of our house, to listen. This was usually an indication that special events were afoot; one night Dreiser talking and the booming laugh of my grandfather; another night Sandburg was humming free verse ballads and strumming a banjo; again our neighborhood mystic and family physician was discoursing on life under Father's prodding. Later the material became a poem in an early book. So it is that many later developments revolved around 4853 Kenwood Avenue in Chicago.

Today the paper headlines read, "Percy Grainger, composer, dies at the age of 78 in New York." He was known for such lilting pieces as "Molly on the Shore," "Country Gardens," and "Spoon River." The latter is a composition I heard for the first time, while sitting on the same stairs after bedtime hours, played by Mother from the score that Grainger had inscribed to Father. It brought to mind the country of the Spoon, and no mistake—it tickled my father mightily. First, because it was named after his immortal book, *Spoon River Anthology,* and, second, because Father was very fond of Grainger. They were good friends but saw little of each other until later years. Grainger had my father's deepest admiration as a man and as a great musician. He was not a composer but a concert pianist, having first appeared at the age of ten, according to this report. He was an Australian, a man of vast courage to live his life for music, regardless of the cost. All of this is in Father's affectionate remark: "Percy Grainger has written a piece called 'Spoon River.' Listen to it."

Affluent Days

At the height of ELM's law practice, about 1913, things were prospering. He was a talented attorney-at-law and for a period of years enjoyed a good practice. His perception to motives, ability to analyze character, cynicism and talent at cross examination, all combined to make him a formidable foe in court. I have often reflected that the combination of these abilities was the catalyst that made his book of Spoon River such a natural product of his pen.

During the affluent days, we lived on the South Side of Chicago in great comfort, had several servants, a cook and second maid (so-called in those days), a janitor, and a yard-man. Commanding the troops was a chauffeur.

In those days automobiles were the exception and not the rule. I have a vivid memory of the long discussion between Father and Mother over the purchase of our first car. The discussion was long and it became rather bitter. My mother felt that there were other things we needed more than one of those things that caused "horses to run away," but Father's imagination finally won the day. He bought a Studebaker, the model was called the EMF 30. Father said that EMF surely meant Every Man's Favorite. Maybe so, but it was a real engineering feat to get the car running. As a result, we hired Edward Fawcett, a self-acknowledged mechanic and chauffeur.

The daily routine of Ed arriving with the EMF 30 from the garage was of great interest to the whole block on which we lived. He would pick up my father every morning at eight to drive him to the 47th Street Illinois Central Station. From here, he took the train to the city after many aggravating attempts to be driven downtown. The car became a part of the family and was used extensively and in turn by all of us. Even Mother became attached to it, and she was happy to be driven to teas, exhibits, and the Corden Club. Many times we took trips over the weekend, driving to Michigan and the Indiana dune country for holidays.

Ed Fawcett became a great favorite of ELM's because of his ability to serve us in a new era, as well as his gracious readiness to do anything that was asked of him. I have heard Father ask his opinion on drinking, gambling, going to church, and many other subjects in which he was more or less interested at the moment. I suspect that he was mostly interested in clowning and used Ed as a foil to pass the time. Edward's answers to Father's many questions always produced great laughter, but he seldom conducted these quizzes with strangers.

The EMF 30 period became an era in our lives. A time of affluence, health, and fun, a time that *Spoon River* became a reality and other works were in gestation. Perhaps it meant more to him than we shall ever know.

Harriet Monroe

The famous *Poetry Magazine* office was at 543 Cass Street on the near North Side of Chicago, a good walk from the Loop. I went there with ELM on several occasions to see Harriet Monroe, the cryptic and talented editor of the magazine. Alice Corbin Henderson, the associate editor, also was a fine friend and poet, who had encouraged ELM's literary efforts over the years. So it was that he felt at home with the editors and advisory committee of the office and enjoyed going there. One of these trips I sat and listened to Harriet Monroe and Father discussing the "poetry crowd" and poems. She was an able critic and commented on his "So We Grew Together" and "They'd Never Know Me Now," among other poems that she liked. Both of these poems are in his book of *Selected Poems* published in 1925 and dedicated to John Cowper Powys, a kindred soul, indeed, and an intimate friend of ELM's. It should be noted here that for a period of ten years or more Harriet Monroe was a fine stimulus for ELM, encouraging him in every possible way. Finally, she was lost to him in 1936, killed in a plane crash in South America. So it came to pass that the world lost a friend of the arts and ELM a literary companion. He said to me one time, "I wish Harriet Monroe could read this poem."

The year 1936 was one replete with trips to New York and many days with Father. He was full of what he termed *visiting* and talked much about the friends and contacts of the time, some of them living at the Chelsea Hotel. On the subject of likes and dislikes of his writing, my notes reflect that Mencken voted for "The Hittites"; Amy Lowell praised "Steam Shovel Cut"; and Sara Teasdale thought that "Neither Faith Nor Beauty Can Remain" was among his finest poems. The poet himself told me that "My Light With Yours" deserved more favorable comment. These discussions took place in New York, Spring Lake, Michigan, Chicago, the Indiana dunes, and a variety of places. They were fascinating. I am thankful that even at an early age I was perceptive and listening in a biographical attitude. I kept a datebook continuously and often upon returning home would sit down and write my recollections of conversations, people, things, and places. For example, John Sloan lived at the Chelsea and was the artist of the illustrations in *Mitch Miller*. I remember so well standing in the window of his studio while he made a drawing of me, page one of the book. ELM said, "You look like Mitch to me, and you are now in the book, my boy." He was highly amused at Sloan's using me for a model.

"Old and Feeble"

My father had a horror of old age—that part of it that brought loneliness and helplessness. He played a game with his two daughters based on this subconscious fear, in which he pretended to be a little boy again. He would pretend and act most realistically the part of a forlorn child. My sister Marcia was called "Dear Grandma" in this drama, and he would plaintively ask her who would take care of him when he was "old and feeble," as he always put it. She would reply, "I'll take care of you, little boy. Don't you worry or be afraid." My older sister, nicknamed Lamb, often played the part of the mother in this game. It was a most popular one during our Kenwood Avenue days. She always gave reassuring answers to the same question from Father.

I regarded this oft-repeated game as silly, and it always embarrassed me when Father played it before my young school friends. I now realize how tragic these episodes were in the light of my father's last two years, when the foolish game became the stark reality.

I use the term *stark reality* advisedly, but with the full realization of some of his traits that baffled me for many years. One was his lack of planning for any contingencies. He saved no money, made no investments, and carried no life insurance. He was a son of the Democratic Party, without reservations in this regard, and prayed that when he was "old and feeble" someone would take care of him insofar as financial support was concerned. Old age comes to all of us in varying degrees of tragedy, but it has always

56

Father and his two daughters, Madeline and Marcia, nicknamed Lamb and Leetle, in 1913.

seemed to me that some provision can be made to pay the expenses and provide a cushion for those who at last are left behind. This thought was not held in favor, and, as a matter of fact, he would not discuss things like life insurance or investments. It was a curious trait of the man who had such a fine sense of law, such successful and able friends, and who enjoyed so much the aroma of the fine wines that came with money.

To run out this theme, let it be noted that, at his death, he left nothing of high value except perhaps the copyright to *Spoon River,* which had been given to me according to Father's letter, but ended up in the hands of his second wife who needed it more than I did. So it came to be that he ran out his philosophy to the end. As the strange cloth was woven, he never changed the thread, although he had several opportunities to do so during his lucrative years of substantial legal fees and, later, royalties on *Spoon River* and othed well-paid writings produced at the top of his power. He may have been prophetic in his scorn of "rainy day" thinking because now we have it to extremes. Some of our youngsters today are more interested in pension plans and titles than ever before, and now is a time when our national government has Father's same disregard for a balanced budget or financial integrity.

The controversial letter referred to is quoted verbatim for the record:

October 31, 1943

Dear Hardin: Your check is gratefully received, you can be sure. In my will I have given you the copyright of Spoon River, which pays about $500 a year. This will indemnify you, but also as head of the house I wanted you to have it. . . .

Your Loving Pa,
E.L.M.

58

Amy Lowell

In the spring of 1915, ELM, in addition to contending with the uproar that the publication of *Spoon River Anthology* had engendered and on which he thrived after years of unrecognized writing, was reading a vast amount of contemporary poetry. One of the writers who came under his competitive research was Amy Lowell. They were friends, and he received much encouragement and inspiration from her.

One of the interesting facets of this friendship was the mutual feeling that several of the writers of this era were exhibitionists, that the arrangement of the type on their poems was more important than the content, that poor work was justified by the color of paper on which the poem was printed.

Be that as it may, the preface to Amy Lowell's *Sword Blades and Poppy Seeds* contains this passage, marked by Father's soft-lead pencil:

> For the purely technical side I must state my immense debt to French, and perhaps above all to the so-called Parnassian School, although some of the writers who have influenced me most do not belong to it. Highminded and untiring workmen, they have spared no pains to produce a poetry finer than that of any other country in our time. Poetry so full of beauty and feeling, that the study of it is at once an inspiration and a despair to the artist. The Anglo-Saxon of our day has a tendency to think that a fine idea excuses slovenly workmanship. These clear-eyed Frenchmen are a reproof to our self-satisfied laziness.

This quotation from her book is significantly appropriate of ELM's feeling at this 1915-16 period toward a large part of the poetry of his contemporaries. Whether it was accurate and justified has been determined by the passage of time, and there is no class of people more critical of each other than artists.

Earmarked for Me

I was attending one of Chicago's better high schools at the time ELM became the Man from Spoon River. He was acclaimed and famous overnight. *Spoon River* not only sold in fantastic numbers for a book of poetry, he was urged to "do it again" and right away. The publishers, Macmillan, had found a new and magic name. Lecture money and royalties poured into the family coffers. Part of this money he earmarked for my education.

We talked again, under the trees at our lovely farm at Spring Lake, Michigan, about my school future. He thought my present school not good enough—"too practical an education." I must prepare myself for Harvard and to do this should attend Phillips Exeter or Andover Academy. It was very shortly obvious that I was going to Exeter. I thought the end of the world had surely come. So it came to be that I was soon on the way to New Hampshire and a new way of life. It proved to be, what I thought it was, a rough experience.

Among my books today I find the *French Reader* by Bierman and Drank, inscribed, "H. W. Masters, 34 Pine Street, Phillips Exeter Academy." This little volume typified my troubles because I wanted to be a civil engineer, not a linguist. If I must take any foreign language, it should be German, not French. All of this drove my father close to fury. It built up a chain of events that became significant to both of us as time went on.

Fairy Stories

In Father's childhood, he had a black dog, breed unknown. The dog was the size of an airedale and had a wavy tail. He called his dog Hohne Boy, and all other dogs we had as a family he insisted on calling by the same name.

When I was a child, Father called me Kaduker. I never was given an explanation for this strange name, but he invariably used this name when disappearing into a drugstore, with the statement, "Wait here, Kaduker, while I get a 'seegar.'" I would wait patiently for his exit and we would continue on our way.

He admired, without reservation, the tales of Hans Christian Andersen and Mark Twain's *Tom Sawyer* and *Huck Finn*. I was started off at an early age on all of them. I must add to this: *Stories from Dickens, Gullivers Travels,* and Robert Louis Stevenson's *Treasure Island*. It was a rich experience for a young boy, particularly under the guidance and warming comment of his brilliant mind. He had one of the finest "book" minds I have ever known.

In my library, among other treasured volumes, is a copy of *Stories from Shakespeare,* retold by Thomas Carter. On the flyleaf is this inscription: "To Hardin from father. My boy, begin now to fill your mind with the beauties of Shakespeare. November 8, 1910." This book and others were my heritage from a wise man when I was eleven years of age.

These were the days of his fairy stories. He embellished the stories already mentioned and often regaled us with his own stories and fairy tales. The animals of his fancy were the Geraufaklus, twice the size of a lion; the Spitzdoodle, a snake with a head like a bear; and that horrific of birds, the Jubjub Bird, as big as a cow but with the talons of an eagle. He told endless stories about these fantastic creatures. His ability to invent new tales, concerning the ferocity of this triumvirate, seemed to be endless.

I look back over the years with affectionate reverence to this man and his love of books, books, books, and more books. We had volumes all over our house, in each room. in closets, and in suit pockets.

I can almost define my father's life span by the character of his reading.

"Be Quiet"

In the original *Spoon River,* published in April 1915, there is a very simple dedication, "To my Wife." It has always seemed to me that those three words were really symptomatic of Father's life up to that time. My mother had, in a manner of speaking, made those three words possible and replete with significance. For had it not been for her sympathy, her protective spirit, and her pride, the book of Spoon River might have remained a small collection of poems, published in *Reedy's Mirror* beginning on May 24, 1914.

The long stairway at our home on Kenwood Avenue in Chicago comes to mind so frequently since Mother's death in 1958. It began its rather tortuous ascent directly outside my father's bedroom and study. It offered a natural method of expressing my exuberance, and I used it as a footrace and shouting area—all of this when Father was away from the house. If he were in residence and working, the slightest noise on my part would bring forth Mother's warning and admonition, "Be quiet! Your father's working." It seemed such a foolish request at the time, but it was typical of all that Mother had given over the years to protect his creative hours. The same consideration was applied to the operation of our household as to cleaning and meals. Father's muse was never banished from his shoulder by the dust cloth or the dinner bell.

Typical of my age at the time was the remark of a pal

of mine, Archie Church, from around the corner. He used to tell our neighborhood gang to go play in Farmer Green's lot because "Hardin's father is writing again." This became an accepted procedure, to move our activities to where noise could reign supreme.

One summer I had the whooping cough and I had it with great gusto and enthusiasm. Although my coughing could not be controlled, it annoyed Father and affected his working hours at home. Consequently, for the good of all concerned, we went to Diamond Lake in Michigan for the summer. Here, my mother, with whole-souled dedication, devoted her days to keeping me on the lake, out of sound of Father's hearing. Of course, this was of wonderful value in finally curing the cough. Mother would start out with me after breakfast in a comfortable rowboat, keeping me entertained for hours.

In the meantime, ELM sat at a kitchen table, placed on the screened porch of our cabin, and tended to his writing. At this time he was doing a group of sonnets. They were written under the name of Webster Ford, 1908-10, and are really not known to any degree within the scope of his later writings. However, the value of the literary effort was always first in Mother's mind. She left nothing undone to protect his time and his mood.

It was not until Father had reached threescore years and ten that he ever mentioned her devotion in this respect. I believe this age brings a sense of reevaluation to all of us when and if we reach it.

Law Office—Chicago

The Marquette Building in Chicago has always been a representative office building. In ELM's day it was one of the best. Here Father held forth at the sufferance of his brother-in-law for a time, who was not one of Chicago's brilliant attorneys—far from it. He was George R. Jenkins, a good, steady plodder. He could evict tenants and collect bills. Nevertheless, my father was between law partners and in the middle of several large lawsuits. Uncle George's offer of office space and services was most acceptable and gave him a certain freedom of action. As is typical of the Masterses, Father took the largest, brightest office and told Uncle George that the smaller office in the suite was surely sufficient for him. George agreed, glad to get more rent and the assurance of some of Father's business.

I worked at this office on Saturdays, running errands, stapling briefs, and doing a thousand things that school boys do in their father's offices on vacation time. It was exciting work for me because it often meant lunch downtown with Father at the Palmer House, a trip to the library, or the rumble of my grandfather's voice when he was here from his law office in Springfield, Illinois.

The thing that comes to my memory, above all else of this time and in this office, was observing Father's terrifying concentration. With law books and references piled high on his desk and table, he was oblivious to the outside world. He brought to his law practice the same imagination and hard work he later brought to his writing. I recall the same out-of-this-world expression on his face when he was writing *Domesday Book*. This interesting book was dedicated to his father: "To my father, Hardin Wallace Masters, splendid individual of a passing species—an American." My grandfather was indeed this and more. He was a fighter for his beliefs, not the expedient politician worried about votes that is so typical of our American scene today. He was the booming voice of the trial court, a man threatened by knife and gun in many criminal cases but fearless in his convictions. I've heard my father say that people on the Sandridge would rather have Hardy Masters defend them than any other lawyer in Illinois.

To digress from law offices for a minute, I cannot help but recall Carl Sandburg's inscription about my grandfather. It is in my autographed copy of *Good Morning America*, and Father wept when he read if for the first time. "Poetry may yet be defined by some phantom who knows and until then these pieces stand as trial shots. . . . Once I drank beer with your father and your namesake grandfather, an oaken man of wide spread. May you live as long as he and like it all."

And so back to the office in the Marquette Building that overlooked the busy, noisy Loop of Chicago that Father loved so well. Compared with New York he called Chicago a provincial city, but it was always his first love.

Eggnog

Much has been said in our family of the indifference of my father to the problems of Mother's family, the Jenkinses. I suppose it is true of everyone's life, that they are indifferent to something—like a mental or soul vaccination. Viewed from the standpoint of another, this attitude of polite inattention to one's relatives can cause much trouble. So it was with my father. He treated some relatives with indifference, not to say scorn. It was not a charming characteristic of his makeup, but certainly a human one.

Let me say that, nonetheless, among my earliest recollections of comments on relatives, was Father's admiration for his father-in-law, Robert E. Jenkins. Although he deemed him a poor lawyer, he admired his Christian virtues and his stout defense of his troubles. My maternal grandfather was caught in the failure of a Chicago bank of which he was a director. He spent some years and much of his none-too-robust physique squaring the debt. From the time my father lived with his father-in-law on the third floor of his home at 4200 Drexel Boulevard until my grandfather died in 1907, I like to believe that they admired and understood each other as men. In those days Drexel Boulevard was a swanky address in Chicago, and the helping hand of a place for the newlyweds to live was long remembered. Lee Masters and Helen, his bride, lived there when I was born. Thus I started on one of the best carriage streets in town, but I did not have my father's luck in living it down. Just recently

This is the house—4200 Drexel Boulevard in Chicago—in which Father and Mother were married. It belonged to my maternal grandfather, Robert E. Jenkins. I was born in this house, and we lived there on the third floor, overlooking the boulevard, from 1898 until 1900.

I took some pictures of this house, both my father's and my first family residence. They are part of this book.

Later on, my grandfather lay stricken with pneumonia in Hanneman Hospital on the South Side of Chicago. He had stayed in Chicago too late one year and the cold, wet winter caught him trying to clean up his desk for a trip south. This was truly a winter of benevolences for ELM. I was told many times by my lovely and devout grandmother, Marcia Jenkins, of Father's devotion to his ailing father-in-law. This took the form of office work, legal briefs, and odd jobs for the family that had been the responsibility of the

69

stricken man. At the last, Father carried the best Hannan &
Hogg Bourbon for my grandfather's daily eggnog. This
errand of mercy, despite Robert Jenkins's hatred of liquor
and the saloon, was in his last days the solace a good
whiskey in moderation can bring. He became, in turn, more
tolerant of the Masterses' enoyment of spirituous *fermenti,*
quail hunting, and other things not associated in the Jenkins
philosophy with Christian living. So it was that the days
went on and ELM kept his father-in-law supplied with the
best bourbon to be had. In addition, they had many wonderful visits as men. I feel sure that Father's practical sympathy
meant much to this sick man.

This may be a rather maudlin and overstressed event in
the overall picture of the poet's human relations. However,
some of them were so understanding or tolerant, particularly
of his frequent disputes with his brother, Tom, and his
beautiful sister, Madeline Stone, even from my adolescent
viewpoint that he seemed to me at times to choose to mis-
understand them. Thus, I try in a manner to balance the
scales with that love which a son must carry as part of him.

Sick Man

"Your father is a sick man," said Dr. Harpole. "I'm afraid he has pneumonia. I'll have to get a nurse in," he added, looking at me as I waited by the second-floor stairs to see what was going on. "You will have to be quiet, son, and make no noise around the house. Complete rest is essential for him the next few days." A great fear tugged at my heart. My father was in bed, sick, an almost unheard-of thing. I could not remember its equal, certainly not since we moved to Kenwood Avenue. Here he was in the sunny, front bedroom, in the big four-poster bed; the shades were drawn, the room dim, and I could hear his hard breathing. He sounded like he was trying to pace the old clock, Tursey Potter, which ticked away on the mantelpiece over the gaslog fireplace.

The doctor said to Mother, "I'll send you a nurse, one that Lee will like. In the meantime, get this prescription filled. Have Hardin take it right down to 47th Street."

That evening, the nurse, Jane, arrived to take care of Father. She was pretty, skillful, and cheerful. She was everything a nurse should be except too pretty to be left alone with even a sick man. In any event, I have always credited her with his recovery and rapid convalescence. He responded to a good-looking woman in typical Masters fashion. It seemed but a few days until he was joking with Jane and having a really merry time. It might be said here that Dr. Harpole was more than a physician: he was a bookman and a psychologist, a most entertaining and wise man. He handled Father's illness with consummate skill.

71

Later on, he told Father that he would never have had the illness if he had been in good shape. As a matter of fact, he had been through many long months of a laborious Will case. In addition, he had been writing most of his time away from the office. He was in one of his periodic times of worrying over bills, household problems, and the inability to get any rest. He was sleeping poorly. So it was, we almost lost him. I think we would have, had it not been for his fine living habits and the care that he normally took of himself. He had a backlog of stamina that came through for him before the days of antibiotics were even in the test tubes of the laboratories.

Mother took his illness in stride, as she did most of life's blows. She was a woman of wondrous courage and fortitude, always cheerful and making the best of situations that seemed almost impossible to the rest of us. She resented the nurse, Jane, toward the last when she felt that Father did not need her care any longer, but for the rest, she carried on for all of us during a pretty grim time. She was short of cash to run the house, which was not unusual because Father had no conception of an orderly financial arrangement. Mother had no allowance or any planned way of operating her household responsibilities. If fees were flush, she had money and he paid all of the bills as she presented them to him. If it was a lean time for him, legal fees not coming in promptly, she had nothing and he paid nothing. This opportunist arrangement left much to be desired and made a vivid impression on me. I thought, as a young man, that money was the most important thing in the world and that my father was to be pitied for not being able to amass a wheelbarrow load of it. I know now that this is an adolescent viewpoint and that to have written one fine poem is more valuable than the biggest bank balance in the world. He believed this, I know, and wrote many poems in the immortal columns, so he was right.

Lewistown, Illinois

Tursey Potter, the Masterses' pacemaker, ticked off the minutes of the somnolent Illinois afternoon. The clock had a lazy rhythm that blended into the heat and inactivity of the day. This might be Lee Masters's last time at the farm for a long while. One of the tragedies of my father's youth occurred, he told me, when he was eleven, going on twelve. He had listened fearfully to a conversation of his parents. "Em, I believe we will be moving to Lewistown before long." These had been horrific words. The tragedy of youth in all its finality; gone his pony, his dog, his beloved grandfather, his gentle, lovely grandmother and her beatific smile. Why move? Why? He thought of the boys of Sand Ridge and the church at Concord and the many fishing trips around the country with Uncle Wilbur. There was another grief— no more loafing with Uncle Wilbur Masters.

He found himself wondering how his grandfather, Squire Davis, had looked in 1830 when he moved to Morgan County, Illinois, from Tennessee. Did he say grace before each meal then or had this custom grown with his worship and love of the Illinois prairie?

The boy's gaze went to the old shelf of medicines that always seemed to cure his Petersburg colds. One special bottle stood out on the shelf: Hart's Honey and Horehound. Many's the spoonful taken from his grandmother Lucinda's hands.

This was my father's story to me en route to Michigan on the boat one starlit night.

73

Tursey Potter—the Masters's pacemaker

According to the records, this house is the first residence of ELM in Lewistown, Illinois. The house was rented by his father, Hardin W. Masters, for a short period of time, . . .

. . . the family later moving to a larger house, off the square (about 1881).

Claudia Perry-Wilson

Although *Spoon River Anthology* is as popular today as it was fifty years ago, others of Father's books seem neglected. Over the years *Spoon River* has probably sold more copies (about 175,000) than any other book of poetry published in this century. It has been translated into fifteen and more languages, has been required reading in English One, and is now enjoying its life on the stage and in the paperback. The premier performance on September 29, 1963, at the Booth Theatre in New York was praised by all seven critics of the metropolitan press.

I have remarked before that my father told me on many occasions that his best book was *Domesday Book,* published by the Macmillan Company in 1920. This was his opinion, but it is not supported by literary historians or the literary critics of today. At least, a search of the clipping books and anthologies of poetry does not help me in establishing his feeling. As a son, I am a biased commentator of his literary ability or his books. However, I can understand that *Domesday Book* came from the pen of a man who loved the practice of law over a period of years. It also is tied into a remarkable family character.

Claudia Perry-Wilson was a black woman of substantial size. She probably weighed over 200 pounds and was a great talker, a great eater, and a most wonderful cook. She used to say that she was "our nigger" and proud of it.

Mother employed Claudia when we first moved to 4853 Kenwood Avenue on the South Side of Chicago and she

Claudia Perry-Wilson was a beloved and devoted member of the Masters household. Cook, literary critic, and counselor of my father for many years, she maintained that Domesday Book *was his greatest work.*

was with us for over twenty-five years. That is, she was with us periodically—my father used to say, "between marriages." Claudia was an uneducated but highly intelligent woman. She knew people. She was both a cynic and a simpleton. She was eternally interested in all of us—our problems, our miseries, and our victories. She raised us and comforted us.

More than this, Claudia was devoted to my father. She understood him and she tried to protect him from himself. His literary fame, as one of the greatest American writers, and his immortality as a poet, became her life. In turn, Father was devoted to her and talked with her by the hour. I can see them on the porch of our Spring Lake farm— Claudia in her rocking chair and Father sitting on the stoop. Occasionally a shrill laugh would come from Claudia or a snort of derision from him as they talked and looked out over the lovely lake. He enjoyed her company and sought her advice on many earthy problems. One of these was *Domesday Book*.

This was the type of poetry she liked, a story she understood, a plot within her own scope of life that she knew from her own area of activity about medical doctors, coroners, and the indifference of love that has gone. So it was that my father talked to Claudia about the situations and about the most realistic treatment of them that came to his mind in connection with *Domesday Book*. I believe that Claudia had much to do as a consultant with the finished product of this epic poem.

Our Kenwood house had a cannel coal fireplace in the dining room. On winter mornings a fire was often burning and snapping for the breakfast hour. Claudia would be moving around the room, her empire, setting the table for her folks. One January morning, a bitterly cold one, with snow feathering down outside the circular casement windows,

I came down early for school. Father sat at the breakfast table, talking to Claudia. He said, "Claudia, I have reconstructed that same circumstance in my new *Domesday Book*. So you agree with it, do you?" I was as contemptuous of his asking her the question as my age permitted. What did Claudia know about books?

The last time I visited this fine woman she laughed and said, "Your father was a great one for pouring sorghum on his corn meal mush. Do you remember that?" "Yes, Claudia, I remember." She died destitute and alone in Cook County Hospital in Chicago, talking to the last about Edgar Lee Masters.

The Black Trunk

In the second-floor closet of our house in Chicago reposed a black trunk. It was the kind that brought to mind the vicissitudes of the nineteenth century. The trunk had a curved lid and the sides were reinforced by strips of wood. In contrast to its feeble appearance, it held treasures for many years that were the subject of much trouble and debate.

Father told me that it contained several hundred poems and a thousand letters from literary people—from Cather to Millay—and critics of his time. Such were the contents and the treasures. After ELM moved to New York in 1923, the trunk became a real heartache. Hardly a month went by that I did not receive a phone call or letter imploring me to send him his trunk. Alas, it was immovable because it constituted collateral to his alimony payments that were in default, the divorce decree having been granted on May 3, 1923.

In addition to the trunk, the house contained the extensive library, over one thousand volumes of his books, all read and collected by him over a period of twenty-five years. Here again, my mother held the books as collateral to the deficient alimony, but to no avail. Finally, in her desperation for funds, the books were sold, some purchased by a Chicago book dealer for a ridiculous sum of money. Rumor has the amount at less than $500, but a fortune to my mother at that time.

The wheel spins on—it is believed the books ended up in the possession of my stepmother, Ellen Coyne Masters. Today, all of the books from Father's original library, except the few in my possession, are owned by the University of Texas. It is said that Ellen Masters received an adequate payment for them. I must add that I'm happy to have them there, available to students and the world, and in the custody of a great university in a great state. My father would have said that the Southwest is the last of America as he knew and loved it. Also he would have added, "So be it."

College Girl

It was snowing and cold, one of Chicago's bleak winter days. The date was December 2, 1923, and I had just put Father on the train for New York.

His departure was the sequel to many days, not to say months, of travail and frustrations. It had been a period when I had desperately attempted to stem the tide of his violent urge to get away from Chicago—from his home, his family, and his friends.

After a futile separation, my parents had been divorced. The stage was set for the new life, and the new wife. The new wife was to be a woman my age who had indeed woven the tough lasso of age for youth. She was a charming girl who attended the University of Chicago—a brilliant student, and a person who had set her cap for my father in no uncertain campaign.

So, it was she who appeared on the scene in New York shortly after ELM's Chicago years, and married him. It turned out to be an alliance of convenience. He gave her a son, and she gave him a sense of security and freedom. I say freedom because in my monthly trips to New York on business during the thirties, I never found her in residence in the apartment at the Chelsea Hotel. He spoke of her with a shrug of the shoulders and the comment, "She was teaching."

The persons of the drama had been many. There were legal friends and associates, from Clarence Darrow to Abra-

82

ham Meyer. There were walking friends, Judge Landis, Sam Morgan, and Bill Slack. There were literary cronies of the time such as Harriet Monroe, Dreiser, Lindsay, and Hemingway. Last but not least there was our family—all involved in the play to various degrees and in relation to their capacities of friend, foe, confidant, or advisor.

As a son I received from Father's lips the score of the game, which side they were on, his or Mother's, and the tenor of the advice or comments he had received in his desperate attempt to get his soul in balance and justify what he planned to do.

The years have softened the episode with understanding and put many of my youthful problems in perspective. I can say that at the time the only friends that approved his actions and strongly supported them were the so-called literary group; the rest did their utmost to persuade him to stay in Chicago and not seek a divorce. I was among the latter group, of course, who felt his departure more keenly than anyone. I was the heartsick son.

Now, as I attempt to reconstruct my thoughts as I return to my home from the railroad station, I am not so sure that the years of his life from 1923 until he passed on in 1950 were not for the best. Many books, some immortal, may have been the reward; only time will tell. The records indicate this period to have been his most creative one.

Boy's Story

For years Edgar Lee Masters had been an admirer and student of Samuel Clemens. He had absorbed most of his books and miscellany, but, most of all, he admired with a passion the Tom Sawyer and Huckleberry Finn stories. I always felt that he compared parts of his boyhood in Petersburg with Tom Sawyer's adventures, and I must admit that the country and environs of that portion of Menard County would stimulate such thinking. The river, the old mill, the drunks, and the mysterious characters were prevalent in the real, as well as in the Mark Twain community of Hannibal, Missouri. In addition to this, the two men had (that is, my father and Clemens seemed to have) a similar kind of humor and came from the same frontier type of ancestors.

It followed quite naturally that, after *Spoon River* had endowed father with an indomitable author's courage, he was ready for a prose book. This one had been germinating in his mind for some years. As a matter of fact, I do not see much difference in the theme of *Spoon River* and the story of Mitch, except in the vehicle of telling.

So it was that in 1920, the book *Mitch Miller* was published by Grossett & Dunlap by arrangement with the Macmillan Company. The illustrations were by John Sloan. He was a competent and sympathetic artist, among a group of father's New York friends. Nevertheless, all things considered and in perspective, the book was not a big success— neither in sales nor from the standpoint of reviews. This was always an item of aggravation and mystery to the author, who stated to me on many different occasions that it was a good book and he could not understand its "missing the mark," as he expressed it. He was at the point in his creative curve where everything that hissed from his pencil was the best. He could not and did not admit a poor book. Later on, when time had mellowed his energy and his point of view, he proclaimed again to me that prose was not his medium but that *Domesday Book* was the best book he ever wrote.

As he requested me to do several times, let me repeat or at least give my layman's impressions of the book at hand— the Masters boy story, *Mitch Miller*. In my opinion, the book was out of key with the subject. It was not a boy's story, as I wanted a boy's story to read and flow. It was as heavy as middle age, not light like fishing on a summer's day. It was, in places, sordid and bitter, not the cruelty of a boy, but the despair of a man. Many of the passages placed Mitch in the position of a person with a man's head on a boy's body. It failed conviction for me as a boy's story. I never liked it. My father sensed this and I felt guilty about it, but could not deceive him, even at the tender age of twenty-one. In fact, I was just an overgrown Mitch and felt that the story should have my understanding and compassion. It didn't, but now I finally understand it. I wish the man who wrote it were here to rewrite it. He had often said to me, "I want to write a good boy's story some day."

Bill Reedy's Gone
1862-1920

For many years prior to about 1914, Father had been writing under the pen name of Webster Ford. He did this with the feeling that it protected his business against prejudice and the mark of eccentricity, which in those days marked the writer. It should be observed here that his nom de plume was also indicative of his concern for the welfare of his family. Furthermore, in those days, I suspect that the success of his law practice came before other things. Writing was definitely an avocation during those early years. Much of his Webster Ford writing appeared in Bill Reedy's *Mirror,* starting with the early issues.

The *Mirror* had a small, but select, circulation. I believe that it was similar to Harriet Monroe's *Poetry Magazine.* Bill never made any money in publishing it and didn't really give a damn about it except for the annoyance of having paper and printing bills to pay. The magazine itself was rather austere. It was about sixteen by twelve inches in size and was printed on a rather glossy white paper in distinctive, but not necessarily attractive, type. In any event, it was a big step in the right direction for the budding author when he was published in the *Mirror,* more especially because it led to the interest and friendship of the publisher.

I recall so vividly my father's asking me to accompany him to Bill's funeral in St. Louis. This was a tragic event for ELM, but also great and important for me. We went to St. Louis on the old Chicago and Alton Railroad—in those days a luxurious ride, fast and dirty. All the way down there, father reminisced about Bill: the fun they had had together, the stimulus of knowing him, what he had done for the unknown writers, and his irreparable loss. One story in particular has never left me, and it came out on this trip. It concerned Bill Reedy's attendance at the funeral services of one of his close friends. Father was along and, to ease their grief, the pair of them stopped at one of St. Louis's many fine old bars. It was summertime and St. Louis was hot. Graveside services were an hour away and the carriage was waiting for them. The beer was cold and delicious, as were the wonderful memories of the departed friend. Reedy and Masters arrived at the cemetery just in time and Bill walked to the edge of the grave to take one last, sad, but reverent, look at the coffin. The edge of the grave gave way beneath Bill's jolly weight and he slid into the grave with the deceased. This story was told many times about old Bill Reedy and always evoked much mirth—in the right places.

So it came to be that this trip to St. Louis and back with my father was a forerunner of many sentimental journeys in which he included me for a period of years. It was my first introduction to the spirit of affection between men of like interests—the same type of camaraderie that made the Marine Corps such a fine body of men. It is hard to delineate, but there was nothing like it in father's life when he had such friends. There were really no ends to his sentimentality. He would literally give away anything he had to old friends at the time of stress, but later become his ordinary cynical self. The friend that had been in peril became the object of good-natured scorn and an object lesson in avoiding doing sentimental things for other people—a strange admixture that the man possessed all his life and caused him much suffering, particularly with the terrible class of people known as "former friends." Can anything be worse than these?

87

Chelsea Apartment

In father's room at the Chelsea Hotel were many books and other items that normally go to make up a bachelor's quarters. I use the term *bachelor* advisedly, because father had a new wife, named Ellen Coyne. She was a brilliant woman, and she had married father perhaps because he was older and famous. I never knew the exact reason and don't believe he did after she had accepted him. In any event, they were not living together all the time at the Chelsea apartment.

The bedroom contained the barest necessities: a brass bed that had belonged to his father, an old trunk, and a hotel chair. In the living room were rather primitive pine bookcases, Beethoven's death mask, a collection of fine old pipes, and his usual tools of the trade—scratch paper and soft-lead pencils. Oftentimes a sketch or a pastel adorned the wall temporarily, the gift of the artist of the month, for he had many friends in the Village and throughout the city.

This little apartment was his home for many of the years that he lived in New York. He went out for his meals and led a perfectly carefree life, to the point of turning off telephone calls at the hotel switchboard when he desired. Many times I was terribly hurt when I called, knowing he was there and could not get through to him. The hotel never violated his instructions on telephone calls.

During the prohibition days, New York was a vast area of fine little bars, and there was always good food—along with the little bars. One such place that pleased him mightily

The Chelsea,
New York

The Chelsea Hotel in New York City was the residence of Edgar
Lee Masters for about twenty years. He wrote in his poem called
"The Hotel Chelsea":

> today will pass
>   as currents of the air
> that veer and die
>   tell me how souls can be
> such flames of suffering
>   and of ecstasy
> then fare
>   as do the winds fare

was the Players Club on Gramercy Park. Here indeed was an oasis for the thirsty artist, and many were the wonderful parties that I attended with father during short visits to the city. One of father's inevitable favorite characters ran the bar for the club, which opened up regularly about four P.M. for the evening's trade. ELM used to say that he "could always get 'er," referring to a drink. He took great pleasure in his cocktails and his damnation of prohibition. He believed it to be a foolish and wicked moral law and said that it could not last. Along with many others, he seemed to relish breaking the law, and, I do believe, he enjoyed his drinks more than after repeal.

I was fortunate at this time to have been with a Chicago investment banking firm that maintained their headquarters in New York. So it was that I came to New York every month on business. On these occasions, we always dined and talked and really enjoyed the city together. I had one *big* problem: it was father's inability to understand why our New York office should make demands on my time. He would pin me down as to the time I could get away from Wall Street and join him. If something in the line of duty intervened, he would be furious with me. On one occasion he left word he could not see me when I arrived at the Chelsea Hotel. It was particularly difficult because he was hard to contact by phone when I would call to say I would be a little late in getting out to his hotel. I realize now that his life alone and his eagerness to hear about Chicago, the city he never forgot, were factors that distorted many incidents for him.

90

The Dream

The white frame house, located at 1501 Holmes Avenue, Springfield, Illinois, is standing today as a nostalgic structure of bygone times. It belonged to my grandfather, Hardin Wallace Masters, and he resided there for a period of years, from about 1912 to 1925. Each day he walked from the house to the terminal of the Spring Street streetcar line and went downtown to his office, enjoying a chew of tobacco on the way.

I visited the house as a boy during the summer of 1914 and have wonderful memories of the time—its activities with my cousins and most of all being with the man adored by his son. The summer was spent in Europe by my father and mother, an extended trip, and this was the reason I escaped parental interference during my own extended visit.

Now the computer hums and flashes, and without intent I recall the vivid twenties and my dream concerning my grandfather Masters. It was one of those curious, potent, unexplainable experiences—a dream. I dreamed that my grandfather was dead. He was calling to me from a small, white barn in back of his house to come and help him. His voice was urgent, powerful, commanding. He must not die, he did not want to leave me, and it was all a tragic mistake. I must help him.

I awoke in terror with his stentorian calls ringing in my ears—soaked with perspiration.

The next morning a wire arrived advising us that he had

been stricken in his bedroom while dressing to go to his law office. A day or two later, after a momentous struggle to survive, he was gone.

A man's life changes rapidly after the loss of his father (1925), and this was a blow of grave consequences for my father. Chicago is closer to Springfield than New York.

Death Mask

The windows on the north side of the white frame house were reflecting the sunshine of the early morning. Hardy Masters was dressing to go to the offices of Masters and Masters, Lawyers, Springfield, Illinois. He was a handsome man, broad of shoulder, keen of eye, and with a head of flowing white hair and a moustache that belied his years.

His black bow tie was obstinate this morning and would not come to form. Suddenly his hand would not obey the lifelong command. A brilliant light crashed into his brain. He fell to the floor of his small bedroom with a moan.

Miles away my phone rang and I heard my father's hard, tragic voice, "Hardin, your grandfather is stricken. Do you want to go to Springfield with me? I wish you would." I did. My grandfather was one of my favorite people, much more so than the average grandfather—hunting companion, storyteller, poker player, just my age but over twice as old.

We met in Springfield, Illinois, father coming from New York and I from Chicago. So it was that an emotional, inspiring experience began that will be in bright windows of my memory for all my years.

My grandfather lay in the simple dignity and peace of the living room of his home on Holmes Avenue. He was more handsome, more eloquent in the great final silence of death than he had been in life. His beauty as an individual created sunlight in the room and seemed to be reflected on the white satin walls of the casket. We were aghast at the

93

scene, in such contrast to the grim fight he made against death. His going had been a long and bitter battle, tragic in his rejection of the decision against him.

Here he was, in the most sublime peace of countenance. We could not leave him.

The fall wind was blowing and moaning around the house. The agonized boughs of the trees in the yard chased shadows over the living room wall and across the patrician face in the coffin. His face, even in the dusk of evening, remained classic in death, and so strong in its American simplicity.

My father had phoned all over Springfield to find a sculptor who could make a death mask, and as the night came it was completed and Hardy Masters lay in state in the living room of his home, surrounded by his family. The street light on the corner, the larger shadows of the limbs moving back and forth on the walls, played a sonata during the rest of the night never to be forgotten.

My cousin, Dr. Thomas D. Masters, and I spent the entire night with our departed grandparent. We knew he had been our father's idol in many ways. He was beloved of his grandsons now sitting by his side. This was the least we could do to honor and revere his American ideals, his courage, and his pagan enjoyment of each day of his life. It seemed to me that he had always taken the good with the bad, much in the stride of a Greek warrior. He had been the epitome of faith in his country, in his family, and in his Kentucky Derby winners. He had lived with gusto and had injected in his son some of the same fortitude to live as his beliefs dictated, with the adjustment to more complicated ways of life and to a more sophisticated time.

The Tribute

The funeral service was held Monday, November 16, 1925, at 1401 Holmes Avenue, Springfield, Illinois, in the living room of my grandfather's home. The Reverend William F. Rothenburger officiated, and the obituary was prepared by my uncle, Thomas D. Masters, my grandfather's law partner. (The quotation is from a memorial book published by the Press Illinois State Register, 1925.)

Subsequently, my father published the Tribute, which he had written in his mother's bedroom that morning after a sleepless night. I quote it from the same memorial booklet for its beauty and simplicity:

In 1859, Thomas Masters died in Morgan County, Illinois, and his son, Squire Davis Masters, wrote simple and moving words in memory of him with all the understanding of a man himself growing old. Then in 1904 and in 1910, Squire Davis Masters and his wife, Lucinda Young Masters died, and their son, Hardin Wallace Masters, did for them what had been done for Thomas. And now I do for this son what he did for them.

He too grew old as they had done before him; and he has left us to grow old and to come to him and to them.

I saw the youth time, the late spring, the June and the full summer time of this father of mine. He was an oak with a thousand glistening and dancing leaves, thoughts and fancies and hopes and delights; and even when his hair was white and his step faltered, his mind and his heart knew no age. Now his body lies before us a withered branch; but as if the storm of death could not touch his unconquered spirit, something of the spring-time greenness remained with him until his breath was breathed forth for the last and all his leaves were cast to the earth. The blow that silenced his tongue and left his spirit fluttering in

95

Hardin Wallace Masters, ELM's father

wonder and in pain did not break the passion of his heart, the eagle clearness of his will; and almost to the end he answered messages of love and care with strong, almost powerful pressures of his hand. Like a vein which pulses till it vanishes, the greenness of the great oak of his life threaded its way to the last tendril of his hold upon this earth; and the spirit of Hardin Wallace Masters strong and clear, tender and just left neither him nor us till the long flight was taken.

Nature is infinite in her power for making men; but so is nature infinite in her will not to repeat what she has once done. No man like Hardin Wallace Masters will ever be in this world again. There were combinations in his spirit so fine and so happy that the chances are infinitely remote of their being repeated.

He had a pioneer ancestry, a pioneer youth that has passed away having contributed the greatest richness that America knows. One part of him seemed to trace itself back to the mountains and the lakes of Ireland, and the village life where the weaver, the blacksmith, the judge, the historian, the king and the poet all dwelt together; and where life was friendship and happiness and not disagreeable labor, care and strife; and where, in a primitive democracy, men loved the harp and loved the hunt, and dreamed of the old ships before the Norsemen harried the seas. And one part of him traced itself to the English blood which loves law and order and justice, and is ready and courageous to fight for old liberties; and is not easily brought to try strange ways and to enter upon sudden departures from old paths.

He was all man in whatever way he be viewed. Everything about his bodily form and strength and courage was of a man. Before he was twenty he was very powerful, lifting more than four hundred pounds with ease, and in all feats of strength—running, jumping, swimming, horseback riding he excelled. Until he was nearly thirty years of age he worked with his hands on a farm. At sixty he was in perfect health and power and had strength then beyond most men at forty; at seventy he tramped as a hunter through the bottoms of Arkansas and around the bottoms of the Sangamon river in Menard county with his boyhood friend, John Armstrong. At seventy-five he was trying cases in the courts, and then physical misfortune befell him and the body would no longer obey the mind and the will; though the mind and the will ruled as they did when he was in the June days of his life.

He never ceased to hope, he talked of returning to his work in the office, and when he could not return his spirit climbed to the sunnier level sent thither by the Celt that was in him; and he planned the renewal of old delights, trips and visits to the very last. He was all man as a spirit, noble and large of mold. His

97

principles were expressions of his nature; they were not cultural acquirements.

He forgot offenses because he could not remember them; they passed from his mind. He hated injustice. He had a genius for being the intercessor, and without reward, and sometimes without gratitude, he gave his time and his money to people trapped in the fate of circumstances.

He was a Democrat, not because he had read history and philosophy and had made up his mind by considering men and issues of the past, but because it was his nature to want all men to have an equal chance in life. He loved people. He loved to talk with them on the public square, to visit with them in the courtroom, or wherever men came together. His contacts were hearty, and of the soil of life, like Lincoln's, like Whitman's, like Goethe's—who found his greatest delight talking with cabmen and workmen. He had no false pride and no pride at all that kept him from doing what seemed the natural thing to do. His tastes, his social perceptions lay along the level of the average life or middle course, and hence his democracy was a matter of feeling and believing with the people at large.

But there was a profound side to his spirit, a subtle and imaginative power to it which left him in the heights; and when he was there I have heard him utter words worthy of anyone who ever lived. None of the Celt in him made him mystical. He saw with lightning clearness everything that entered into his life and surrounded it. And this keenness of intuition gave him unusual understanding of men, of political parties and those events in life where the changes take on the aspects of the charmed problem. There was the strong salt of the practical in him in his judgment. His love for liberty, his understanding of liberty were pearls thrown away in this day of change. But he never altered his attitude towards liberty or toward democracy for the reason that he was never discouraged. He had a genuine genius for the law—that genius which knows what the law is because it knows what it should be. And in the early days of his practice he carried through many notable cases involving the application of old principles to new conditions, which showed the genius and originality of his mind. As a lawyer he was never discouraged. Any case could be won that he had, and if he lost one it could still be won if tangles could be lifted so that he could go on or up.

In his going about the country, traveling the circuit, he had collected the greatest fund of anecdotes, stories of men, stories of his old friend Herndon, with whom he was in law partnership, and stories that Herndon and others had told him; and each one of these stories was racy or humorous, and all had a telling point. His memory for these things was marvelous, and even at the last

98

he did not repeat himself, but always had something new to tell.

It is a source of the greatest happiness to me that age never touched the essential part of his spirit. An era of the law business passed with him. It is not stories now, and not speeches, and not first principles and originality, and not justice coming out of the thought and feeling of a democracy gathered into a box of twelve men; but it is a system in legal mechanics, as a part of the vast machinery which runs the imperial commerce of the world.

This new era came upon him like a change from guns to gas might come upon an old general. He may have thought that he was failing, just because he had no intellectual pride and no great belief in his own gifts. But it was not he that was failing; it was the new age which had dawned twenty-five years ago, and was coming to its noon.

He was one of the clearest minded and most sensible men I have ever known, he was the most truthful man I have ever known. He consulted expediency and his own advantage less than any one I have ever known. He had a courage both physical and spiritual beyond any man I have ever known. He was a rare combination of play-boy, strong man, story teller, hard-liver, keen lawyer, democrat, stroller, talker and laugher through this world, hopeful that democracy would finally win, that life would work out well enough, if not for the best; but always that life was wonderful and not to be surrendered until the full allotment of years, because there was so much to do, to enjoy and to live for.

If before coming into this world I could have chosen my father and chosen him with all the understanding that I have today, he is the man that I should have chosen for my father. Whatever I have inherited from him in strength or health, or gifts or understanding of life, I count as more precious than all the riches of the world.

Whatever his belief was about creeds, it never occurred to him to doubt that there was a power that sustains and moves through man and through the universe. He gave this matter no more thought than he gave thought to the existence of his own father. With him there were basic things from which we start and upon which the mind rests. And as in politics he was democratic, striking the average level of thinking, in religion he was practical and of common sense—even as some of the greatest minds have been, leaning neither to doubt on the one hand, nor to mysticism and credal tangles on the other. He believed in and practiced the cardinal principles of Christianity, and it never occurred to him to analyze them, or to look for anything better. They were the expressions of his nature which was mainly forgiving, generous and devoted and loving, both in his private and his public life.

If democracy on earth was a goal to strive for, immortality with him was a democracy too, to be shared in by all, with the rule of cause and effect working elsewhere and always as it does on earth. It did not fit in with his ideas of justice or goodness that any of these blind and struggling millions on earth would be shut out from a democratic chance of immortality.

Father and Friend, as the pressure of your hand told us to the last that you understood our love and returned it to us, so let it stay in our hearts as a symbol of your thought of us wherever you are, even as we send to you lasting memory of all that you were from youth to age.

The last paragraph should be of interest to those biographers who have said to me, "Wasn't your father an atheist?" To such I continue to say, "No."

Grandfather's Lincoln

Tom Evans, our cashier, came by my desk and said, "Here you are, Bub, a letter from Springfield," and tossed it on my desk.

My grandfather, inspired I believe by my father's fame as an author, had been working on a book about William H. Herndon. He had known the bearded Herndon intimately around Petersburg and later as an associate in law cases that they worked on together. Herndon had told many interesting stories about Lincoln and later became one of his biographers (1888).

It had been my part as a grandson to discuss the material with my father at an opportune time and to find a publisher.

To this end I had several discussions with my friend, the late Ralph Fletcher Seymour. He was a publisher of exquisite books—using his own special type and designing the entire volume. Seymour was a fine artist and did all the art work for his publishing business. He was, of course, deeply interested in the subject of Lincoln and in anything that ELM's father might do, particularly so as a small publisher that was alert to getting that first "best seller."

Well, the letter was from author Hardy Masters. I always found excitement in the letterhead: Masters and Masters, Lawyers, Springfield, Illinois. Frequently such letters carried an invitation to go quail hunting, but not this day. Dated April 15, 1925, it said:

101

Dear Hardin: Yours at hand. Thanks. I have concluded that if you have not closed for the sale of the Herndon article when this reaches you that you may withdraw it from the market and return it to me at once as I am not satisfied with it. And that I can rewrite it and make it different and in several ways much better and much longer. I think then it will be easy to either sell or have it printed in pamphlet form. What do you think? We plan now to go to Maine for the summer but have not definitely determined.

Affectly your Grand Father
H. W. Masters

I walked over to Michigan Boulevard to Seymour's office in the Fine Arts Building to show him the curious letter. We sat in his studio on top of the Fine Arts Building, looking west over the great city of Chicago. He said, "This view reminds me of Paris when I was living in a small studio room but not starving to death," and he laughed. I said, "Ralph, this view reminds me of Chicago in April and that I am a poor publisher's agent."

The manuscript was returned to my grandfather as requested. He died six months later and the Herndon material was never seen again to my knowledge.

My father said, "It wasn't the first lost manuscript in the family. Perhaps it was all to the good," or familiar words of his to that effect.

Poplar Tree

There are so many memories of the two who gave us life. It is difficult to sift them and present valid pictures that reflect a man's soul and his longings. My father was often difficult to interpret. His moods were kicked off by so many physical, as well as mental, impacts. For example: he was responsive to winning a lawsuit and planned what he would do with the fee, often before it was received. He was expansive on these occasions—he bought a new suit, took a trip, came home with gifts for the family There was this— he never could save or put away money for a rainy day, and later, as a poet, he had rainy days.

We had a very comfortable front porch on our Kenwood Avenue house. He loved June in Illinois. I see him sitting on the porch, smoking his inevitable pipe. It is after dinner and the predarkness mood has him dusk dreaming. Suddenly there is a whisper of wings and a night hawk sails by, uttering his forlorn cry, which father described as the dusk call. He would shake his head and sigh. One of the family might say, "What is the matter, Lee [or Father]?" Often there would be no answer except a blank stare from dark eyes. He was writing.

A stone's throw to the north of our house was a poplar tree. It was a beloved tree to Father and part, I believe, of the melody of the night hawk's cry. The June breeze

103

This is the South Congregational Church at 40th Street and Drexel Boulevard in Chicago. The minister was Dr. Willard Thorp, and this was the only church that Father attended during his Chicago years. He was devoted to Dr. Thorp and participated in church activities for as long as Dr. Thorp remained there.

Edgar Lee Masters in Vermont, 1937

ELM and A. M. Sullivan in July 1942

This is the Edgar Lee Masters Memorial in Petersburg, Illinois. The house was built in 1870 and was located at 528 Monroe Street. It now stands, as shown above, at 8th and Jackson Streets.

The Masters clan. Top, left to right—Dr. Carl Stone, Hardin W. Masters, Emma Jerusha Masters, Edgar Lee Masters; bottom, left to right—Madeline Masters Stone, daughter Elizabeth Stone, Lucinda Masters, Squire Davis Masters, and Helen Jenkins Masters.

would rustle the poplar leaves and father would again start and sigh to himself. He was a man locked soul-wide to many incidental moods of nature and many night hawks and many trees. I mention these vivid incidents as examples of his rapport. I believe he actually suffered something akin to pain for the unfathomable beats of the world's music—at the dunes, on the porch, crossing Lake Michigan. It made no difference. Once he tuned in, he suffered. I understood this train of thought and I look back and feel that he knew I did.

Let us flash back to another part of the film. The picture is our little twelve-acre farm at Spring Lake, Michigan. Father loved this farm and he loved the blue and gold state of Michigan. Great would be his scorn today at the state's financial travail and the stupid people who have reduced its once proud independence.

The picture is a small vegetable garden down a woodsy road to the rear of our house. The poet is honing a scythe and peering intently at his work. His worn grey hat is on the back side of his head. His clothes are those of a weekend farmer. It is hot, and he loves the sweat that drips from his arms. He hears the voice of the lake and the silent afternoon talk of the crows. He is getting physically tired and he is very happy. On his mental slate are a poem and a legal brief, which had been without the desired solution. These are solved by his exercise, and the grass falls again under the strokes of his scythe. Many problems were solved by the man in this manner. I repeat, he loved his farm and he loved his ability to work as he had as a boy on his grandfather's Illinois prairie.

Sam Morgan

Samuel Morgan lived on the third floor of our Chicago house—he was an elite boarder. The friendship with ELM was well glued together by strong literary interests, Morgan being among the best read men my father had known at the time; in addition, he was in need of friends, which always appealed to lawyer Masters. He was the head of a firm of court reporters, played the piano, was violently opposed to Catholics, and had other diverse traits of character that made him attractive and unusual—different. I walked with them many miles, listening to their conversations on Goethe, Sandburg, the pope, and Jack Powys, to name a few. Much of the talk would be ribald and often hilarious, once in awhile acrimonious to the point of bitterness.

So it came to be that Sam Morgan thus became a family friend; my sisters adored him, and Mother numbered him among the better influences of my life. He was also a stabilizing influence on Father, for he tended to keep him out of the extremes of feeling and opinions that often caused him so much trouble and unhappiness. In any evaluation of friends this man would deserve much consideration. His likes and dislikes were similar to those of my father, he loved to walk, to read, to talk, and to act as a foil and balance wheel. He came into Father's life at a time when each man needed the other. Morgan was getting a divorce, his first world gone, and he was lonely and needed sympathy. ELM, Sam Morgan, and I spent many weekends together.

Later, my father was in the same marital situation but had no Sam Morgan to back him up. The fact was that Morgan took my mother's side of the problem and openly disagreed with my father's decision and actions. Typical of Morgan's thinking was his comment on Maeterlinck's book *Death*: "This author's books are forbidden by the Hierarchy of the Roman Catholic Church to the members of that Institution in this, the Enlightened Age of our Lord 1914"—I remember my father's saying to him, "Tut, tut, Sam, you will fry in hell, and don't call on me because I'll be busy too."

Soft-Lead Pencil

Father was careless in his dress, not to the point of buying cheap clothing, but just careless. His grey flannel suits were always loose fitting and unpressed. Obviously, clothes were just something to be put on, a bothersome necessity. His neckties were always askew and tied loosely. He would ignore haircuts for long periods of time.

In contrast to clothing was his immaculate physical appearance. I cannot recall him unshaven or with anything but clean hands and nails.

I shall always associate the shavings from a soft-leaded pencil, pipe ashes, and rough scratch paper as his marks. One or all of these could be found in any room he had used and, of course, with it, the fragrance of a well-smoked pipe.

To construct a proper biography, I believe one would have to formulate a mental chart, based chronologically on the large areas of his life. For example, he was forty-five years of age when the Spoon River image was born. What were the colors of his canvas during the next ten years? This was the pre-New York period—bitter, tragic, and perhaps never to be fully related. Then about 1925, he came into a joyous, fruitful period, living in New York among admirers and other artists. This was the Chelsea Hotel period. Here in his modest quarters—living room, bedroom, and bath—his writing came of age. A small table was placed before his living room window, and on this he labored each day. The view was a small fenced yard, containing one

110

starving ailanthus tree. Beyond this, the red brick wall of another building. Inspirational? No, but its very drab brutality seemed to urge him on.

Many, many hours I spent in this room, visiting with him. It was here he declared that *Domesday Book* was his greatest. It was here we marked up his books of poetry with dots and dashes—my best choice and his. It was here he visited with Dreiser and Sandburg and many others of the absorbing literary era that had come to New York from all over the country.

This was in the 1930s and in my father's sixties. I would say, however, that the sixties were his years of power. A slowly aging man, like all the Masterses, he was formidable, mentally and physically, but particularly in his capacity to enjoy life.

Chicago

Chicago, my birthplace, is a lovely city, in addition to being a dirty one. This is a strange statement, but true. It is a city of great contrasts and of violent and contrary moods. To those of us who love it as a great city, there is understanding. I think of the corner of Jackson and Michigan in wintertime, with a north wind blowing people around the corner in bitter cold. I think of Michigan Boulevard on a June day with the lake, a shimmering jewel, and soft June clouds sailing past the tower of Illinois Central Station at 12th Street. I think of its industry, its art, its music, and the indomitable spirit of the old families. I also must think of it in August, with the thermometer in the nineties and the humidity almost unbearable. ELM often discussed with me Chicago's moods in identical terms.

The lawyer-poet wrote a book about Chicago, named *The Tale of Chicago*. It was dedicated to me and published in 1933 by Putnams. It is not one of his great books. It just missed, like so many things do under artistic hands that are under pressure. I say this with reservations, as a businessman and not as a literary critic. However, I have talked to so many admirers of father's works who never heard of it, that I believe my judgment is borne out by the book's lack of appeal and sales.

Nevertheless, here is the great, sprawling giant of the world named Chicago, where father started his legal career collecting bills for the People's Gas Company. It was all that

112

came to hand for the country boy who had passed his bar examination on his own and arrived to make his mark. In any event, the book on Chicago sets the posture or perhaps atmosphere of many fine years of his life.

My earliest recollection of the demands of business on him came when we lived on Ellis Avenue, second floor north. Once in awhile I was permitted to go over to the 43rd Street Station of the Illinois Central to see the trains that Father took to go to the office, "to make money," he said. I would duck a shower of cinders, listen with awe to the local steam engine, and wonder why men couldn't go down to the office in boats and avoid all the noise and dirt.

"Going to the office to make money" became one of the oft-repeated phrases of Father's life. I have seen him leave and return in snow, cold, heat, rain, and in every personal mood—almost matching the seasons; and always without serious complaint, except for the utter boredom of the daily project, which finally not even his transient reading could overcome. I would suffer like a kicked dog when on a particularly bad day Father would close the front door, saying "Well, goodbye, Kaducker," following a reasonably good explanation of his departure. At the time it seemed curious that he always made that comment. Later on, having spent a few years growing up, I understood his sighs and the torture of his position.

Then there were a succession of Loop office buildings. The Monadnock, the Marquette and the Portland Block, the office shared with Bill Slack: each, in turn, a portion of the man's life that became so important in his relative reactions to living. Perhaps his life is well expressed in a series of buildings. Why not?

Clarence Darrow

Having been born in Chicago and having lived there most of my life until I was in my early fifties, I received many complaints, questions, letters, requests, and other items from various people, which I imagine may always fall to the lot of the elder son of a famous father.

Some of these occasions and inquiries were most pleasant and others disagreeable. My father always hated the *Chicago Tribune* with a fine and fervent passion. He lost no opportunity to ridicule its editor Colonel McCormick and his editorial policies. He compared the paper with gusto and disparagement with the *New York Times*. He believed the *Times* to be the finest newspaper in the world. All of this, of course, did not help his local law practice, his writing, or his family. The *Tribune,* in turn, never let up on the Masterses, and it had a delicate but fatal way of driving people out of the city. According to one story, the unrelenting enmity of the *Tribune* caused, in one way or another, the illness of a number of prominent citizens who were unfortunate enough to disagree with Chicago's controlling newspaper.

Be that as it may, over the years I caught much of the backwash—particularly after ELM moved to New York in 1925, after the bitter and futile divorce proceedings against my mother. I say futile because he had fine attorneys, some sympathy to the actions, much understanding, but he went too far. He got his divorce but also received wounds from which, in my opinion, he never recovered. One of the old infield who took offense was Clarence Darrow, his former law partner. Darrow admired my mother with great sincerity and tried to be tolerant and sympathetic to both my parents. This was too much for even a man of his breadth. The result was my father's silent bitterness, and later, open enmity.

So it was to my great surprise one blustery March day in 1930 that I received a call from Ruby, Mrs. Clarence Darrow. She called me to discuss father's refusal to answer any questions or assist in any way with Darrow's biography. This was typical of my father and of the many contacts I had with a past with which I was not always familiar. It was typical of Edgar Lee Masters because, when he once made up his mind that he was through with a friend, philosophy, book, painting, or piece of music, he was really finished with him, her or it. I have never known a person who could cut a piece of himself, *excise* is the better word, and never even admit a scar. This was one of his most terrifying traits of character and one that I am just beginning to understand for him. Suffice it to say, insofar as the Darrow biography was concerned, he had never heard of the man. Would I act in Mrs. Darrow's behalf and, as a son, plead with him to make available his facts about a great man for posterity? I told her that I would, but that I would fail.

It may be recalled here that Father was instrumental in getting off his partner, Darrow, when he was charged with bribing a jury in a famous labor trial, the McNamara case of 1911. Father's legal brain and ability to brief the pertinent law won the day for Darrow. Neverthless, it was the end of the partnership. I have my suspicions that my father

115

felt that Darrow withheld facts about the case that he was not aware of at the time. He would never say so, but I always believed that he would not have defended Darrow had he known the complete story at the time. Maybe Darrow knew this too.

Ironically enough, there is no mention of his law partner, Edgar Lee Masters, in his biography published by Scribners in 1932.

I'll Meet You There

In 1919 the Thomas D. Masterses, ELM's brother and his wife, had rented a house on Woodlawn Avenue near the University of Chicago for a period of months. It was told that is was from this vantage point that my father courted his second wife, Ellen Coyne. Ellen was at this time attending the University of Chicago and was about 20 years of age—a glamorous conquest for a man in his fifties, not even up to French standards of half-your-age-plus-seven. Nevertheless, I have often felt that Ellen was more mature than my father in promoting this alliance. She knew exactly what she was doing, under the guise of being carried away by an older man's attention. More to the point, America's famous poet of the moment was compelling to Ellen, to my way of thinking. At any rate, here sat my father in the Masters house, waiting for Ellen's classes at the University to be dismissed so that he could see her. And she graciously complied with his wishes by stopping each day at the house to see him or as a starting place for other social activities. She fed his loneliness with a skillful hand, aided and abetted by others who understood his domestic situation, and the term *understood* is used advisedly.

The Vice-President

Charles Gates Dawes, vice-president of the United States under Calvin Coolidge in 1924, was a distinguished and able banker in Chicago. He was a friend of ELM over the years and we all admired him. What my father had in common with this astute, conservative man of business, I'll never know. I do know that Charlie Dawes, by his attention and advice to him, made life easier and certainly displayed friendship and admiration for the lawyer and man of letters. Nevertheless, it was a curious friendship to me, and I mention it again here as such. Charlie Dawes gave me my first job, at ELM's request, and his friend, Averill Tilden, taught me the bond business. For this experience I am eternally thankful to my sire because I have loved the investment banking business all my life. However, my choice of vocation was a disappointment to ELM. He believed that I should have been a lawyer or a medical doctor. He did his best to give me the education and background for a legal career, but, being as smart as all young men, I looked at his professional striving and wanted no part of it.

Last Law Office

Despite the affectionate counsel of friends, of myself, and of others, Father pushed on to the necessary tragedy of cutting himself adrift from his natural environment in Chicago. At the time I did not understand it as I do today, but the elements of the Jenkins-Masters traits were present. Bill Slack took the law business that came to the office in ELM's absence and, according to my father, never mentioned it until the fee was paid. In addition, Slack dunned him for the office rent and, it appears, took advantage of Father's many absences from their little office. Recently I visited this old office building, Portland Block, in the beauty of a June night. I gazed up at the windows that my Father, poet-lawyer, must have looked out with bitter contempt because of a lawyer friend who had turned against him in his travail.

Alice Davis

My father had lived in New York for about ten years when he met Alice Davis. The period from 1935 to 1938 was marked by her care of him, her understanding, and the work she put in on his manuscripts and literary activities. She has written a book entitled *Evenings with Edgar,* which deserves to be published so that it may become a part of the story of the man to whom she dedicated four years of her life. The manuscript is over 500 pages long and displays dignity and understanding in the telling. Some day, it is hoped, Alice Davis may have it published.

In the meantime I tell, as best I can, my recollection of talks with ELM, from memoranda prepared at the time, of some of the highlights of his period at the old Chelsea Hotel.

This decade, 1930-40, in New York must have been exciting and stimulating times to the creative people. My father was no exception despite a blasé attitude to the contrary. He would talk a bit about Havelock Ellis's book, *The Dance of Life,* returning to laugh about a trip to Baltimore to see Mencken. Another afternoon over a Scotch he talked bitterly of our venture into imperialism and its destructive force on America. He had voiced his opposition to it with his play *Maximilian,* he said.

Several weeks later he described visiting William Jennings Bryan at the Willard Hotel in Washington during the convention. Father's political interest was short-lived but in scope went from Jefferson and ended with his disappointment in Bryan.

ELM had a strong affinity for Greek classical literature.

He repeatedly went through Plato, and as early as 1909 was collecting and reading the Bohn Library books such as *The Comedies of Aristophanes,* and *Suetonius' Lives of the Caesars.* One beautiful moonlight night he sat in our living room at the Spring Lake, Michigan, farm and tried to interest me in the story of Helen of Troy. He had a fascinating voice, deep, melodious, softly commanding; he was a good reader. Perhaps poetry was his best vehicle, but my thoughts were not with him on this occasion except to be flattered by his time—the murmur of the waves on our shoreline helped to distract me as well.

Also, during this decade he was working on his book on Walt Whitman and his autobiography, *Across Spoon River* (1936). It was a busy, most productive time for him, 1930-40, and it reflected the stimulus of important companionship and contacts.

The sequel is that Dexter Masters and I were invited to the old Chelsea Hotel within the last few years to see Alice Davis (Mrs. Charles Tibbetts), who has resided there now for many years. It was here that she first met father, in the early thirties. This friendship went on until his last illness. She has many of his autographed books, letters, and a few manuscripts. His letters and books she has given to the New York Public Library at the suggestion of H. L. Mencken.

There is no question about her love for Father and that she was a protective and happy influence for him at his hotel. She told us that Ellen Coyne's story, given to *Time* magazine at the time and depicting Father in dire need, was a strange fiction. Alice told us that Father had received his Macmillan checks on time and had several thousand dollars in the bank.

She has been a concerned and devoted friend to all of us over the years since ELM died. Alice Davis must be considered a significant part of his Chelsea years.

121

Son Hilary

It will be twenty-six years this October since my father lay in bed at a rest home in Elkins Park, Pennsylvania. Fortunately, out of his more than eighty years of life, he spent only two in ill health and actually incapacitated. It was not my good fortune to be near him in those years of his last illness, but his wife, Ellen, served him well.

All of us took the position that in her he had an energetic, young wife with a good teaching job and that she would take care of him. She had made her bed, now let her lie in it, in a manner of speaking. Suffice it to say, it was a practical and realistic arrangement and one that pleased all concerned at the time. My half-brother, Hilary, was more of a problem than his father and caused his mother, Ellen, more worry. The fact is, nevertheless, that Hilary seemed to be just another boy with Masters characteristics. He was not bad or unkind, but just full of the strong prairie wind of Illinois. I knew because I had been through it all and could have been of help to him.

My father was very fond and proud of his younger son and always predicted big things for him. With it all, he acknowledged that the boy might be a "little wild but would steady down." He felt that Hilary someday would be a famous writer and hoped that life would give him the time and background for his work. He often said to me, "Watch out for your half-brother, Hilary; he is a fine boy." This comment always gave me a heart twist because he had so

122

often said to me, "You are a good boy." Well, his two good boys are now miles apart—physically, mentally, spiritually, and out of touch at a time when they should be together as brothers of the blood.

Father would have been both amused and saddened at the trick of time in relation to his sons. I can hear him almost to the word make one of his bitter, cynical comments about the foolishness of life and the inability of people to control it. He would have laughed and made a peculiar hissing noise with his mouth to add his peculiar emphasis to his pity or scorn, as the case might be. He might have said, "After all I have been through with my mother and sister, to think I have sons who have no more sense than to commit the same folly of indifference and neglect." As I write these words, I know that he would say this to both of us.

Little Porch

On a memorable trip to Central Illinois with my father in September of 1940, we visited all his former haunts: cemeteries, churches, and the homes of old friends of several generations. Also several saloons.

Father grew up in the traditions of the Lincoln country and loved to recount that President Lincoln had tried cases in the yard of his grandfather's farm, when on the circuit as a young lawyer, under the trees and away from courtrooms.

On this trip we spent considerable time in his boyhood town of Petersburg. One morning, after a thorough walk around the town square and numerous inquiries like "What happened to old Lucian Smith's boy, Homer?" to many of the astonished loiterers on the square, we proceeded to the first house Father lived in in Petersburg.

This house was located at 528 Monroe Street. It was modest in the extreme and, as he put it, "cold as hell in winter and hotter than that in summer." It had stove heat and no running water, but the view of the rolling hills of the countryside was good and it was comfortable to the times. Here the poet lived from about 1870 until the family moved to Lewistown in 1880. Despite the modesty of the home and the privations of the family—compared to modern day standards—it was a cherished place.

On this occasion my father stood on the little porch, lost to the looks of the people around him, and looked out over

124

the town. Smoke was curling up the valley from breakfast fires, and the color of fall in Illinois was over the land. He was muttering great lines of poetry, somnolent and rhythmic lines that sounded as soft as the day. I said, "Father, what did you say?" "My boy, that is from Homer, the *Iliad*, it goes almost as far back as this house." I have never forgotten this humorous statement as we stood on the porch he had lived in over sixty years past.

We visited a saloon on the square and had a bourbon. Here again was the pain of revisiting and the calling up of old and dear images. He said to me, "Your grandfather had many a drink over this bar and what a man he was when he was State's Attorney. He was fearless and strong, quite a man before a jury." So, we relived his youth over and over again on this memorable trip, to the point where I believed that I had been there with him; in fact, that I had been one of his boyhood pals. So it was, he used a strong and vivid brush on the years that had intervened. This was not New York; friends at the Players Club had heard, but I had been there. I felt that day as if I had actually played with my father before I was born. I stress again his creative ability for times and places and stories, and, above all, his love and admiration for his father and grandfather.

Central Illinois

I have been working on this biographical sketchbook for a period of several years and am not happy with it. Once in a while, as I've turned my thoughts on and off, a vivid vignette has come rushing along, but in the main, it seems a very simple and basic piece of work to date.

However, one feature comes to focus when I review the pages of my efforts, and that is the repetitious emphasis which I have unconsciously placed on the Petersburg years. The Menard County days, the years of father's youth, his grandparents, and their influence on his whole life predominate in my thinking. The reason, I am sure, is the number of times I have heard ELM in some forty years of vivid association speak of these years in that Central Illinois country. He described Petersburg as his "heart's home."

In contrast, he spoke very little about the white house, with the strange three-story cupola, in which he lived in Lewistown, Illinois. This is the house that was his home from eleven years of age until he moved to the city. This is the house that should have filled his memory with the days of his youth. Nevertheless, as I have pointed out, his stories always went back to Petersburg, to the days on Squire Masters's farm, to the days when Lucinda made graham gems for him, and to the days of fishing and hunting with his Uncle Wilbur Masters.

Another factor in this preoccupation with his early years is most evident in his works. A topical examination of his

126

poetry will reveal the impact of the early years. His mind always ran to the Sand Ridge, Concord Church, the Sangamon River, the Old Mill, and other sentimental places of his days in Menard County. This is most interesting to me in attempting to give a son's picture of his father. As a matter of fact, are not these the primary motivations for *Spoon River Anthology*? Would these poems have been written without his obsession for the country and its people? The answer, I believe, is self-evident. Father's very unusual remembrance of his early years later produced the genie that whirled through the lines of "Slip Shoe Lovey" and "Lucinda Matlock." Thus life progresses within us in reels of beauty, stored for a future use.

Room 214

The old cage elevator at the Chelsea Hotel creeps upward to room 214, and I cannot help but shudder as the years turn backward. So many times I rode this cage with high anticipation of a visit with Father. He was beloved of all the black help around the hotel, and there was always a joke or a comment from the elevator operator. "Your Dad told me that—*snicker* . . . *laugh*—that you was a hellion when you were younger, that you caused trouble up at the place in Michigan." My rejoinder was, "Just a chip off the old block," and then much laughter. Sometimes a serious remark, "Your Dad ain't a'eatin' too well" or "He's been a'pinin' for home folks." Always the elevator reached father's second floor too soon to continue all the reports that were proffered, but there was the affection and love that only the blacks bestow on the people they cherish.

How many nights had father come up on this lift, elated or despondent? Here was a world within a world. Here was his world of creation, his Spartan room, his writing table, his dismal back yard, his reference books, his life. Above his quarters, a floor or two, was the life of Alice Davis, the lonely, strange, understanding woman who eased his pain caused by the separation from his Chicago life after he arrived in New York.

Just recently I read parts of a biography that she had written about her companionship with father, starting about 1933 and running at full tide until 1938. This is a strange, beautifully innocent, but also cynical, account of these years. You do not doubt her sincerity or her veneration of the poet, but certainly you have to give her credit for intruding into the life of a man for the purpose of diversion: the reflection on her of his genius.

Ah well, one of these days the Chelsea will be torn down. There will not be a vestige of its memories or its shabby appeal. The voices of the elevator operator will be silenced and the top floor will not house the ubiquitous Alice Davis. So it is, I was glad to reopen old wounds a few months back on a trip to New York.

This picture of Edgar Lee Masters was taken at the Chelsea Hotel by A. M. Sullivan on Father's seventieth birthday.

New York, N. Y.

"New York is the cultural capital of the country," ELM had told me in 1923 when he was getting ready to move there. In 1936-37 his coterie of distinguished and famous friends proved his point. Dreiser, Mencken, Wolfe, and others provided a constant menu of delectable conversations and inspirations. Be that as it may, he had little enough money for entertainment. Meals, eating around the city, were expensive even in those days. Over the years he was a great admirer and friend of Theodore Dreiser, whom he called "Dee" on occasion, and the two authors were visiting back and forth. He thought Dreiser's *Sister Carrie* one of the best novels of the time (1917). Dreiser had published fifteen books, and this inspired ELM to do more work on the novel as a vehicle for his poetic talents, and according to father's comments, Dreiser had places in the country, away from the heat and noise of the urban apartment, where it was discussed. In my library is a first edition of Dreiser's *The Titan* inscribed to ELM as follows: "To Edgar Lee Masters with good thoughts from Theodore Dreiser N. Y. May 28, 1914." I have pasted in the front of the book this letter:

165 West 10th Street
New York City

Dear Masters   May 28, 1919
   I am once more up though not "around" very much.
Two broken ribs, a sore arm & a sore head appear to be
"about all." My ribs are done up in sheets of adhesive
and a belt. So its hard as well as uncomfortable to move.
But here's thanks for your telegram & letters. I'm
supposed to be around again in 4 or 5 weeks.

Dreiser

There was this friendship nurtured in New York, but in
the spring of 1937 there were other compatible souls. ELM
was fond of Ridgley Torrance and spent time with him.
There was also a young poet named August Derleth from
Wisconsin—"A bright young star on the horizon," he wrote
me. He suggested that I might enjoy "Hark on the Wind";
he lauded it—a fine poem.
   The cost of living was temporarily overshadowed by an
emotional problem—"clouds gathering on the horizon
again," although he had done his best to keep them away
from his work at room 214, The Chelsea. H. L. Mencken
was a fine stabilizer for him and he visited him in Baltimore.
He loved Mencken's brazen contempt of living-room sensi-
bilities and his genius for the scalpel-sharp phrase. The two
men dined frequently in New York at Luchow's restaurant
to discuss the temporary scene of letters. I feel sure that
Vachel Lindsay, Robinson Jeffers, Zoe Akins, Edna St.
Vincent Millay, and others came in for their comment.
   In 1938 Thomas Wolfe, a resident of the Chelsea and a
frequent visitor of ELM's died at Johns Hopkins Hospital.
I was in New York in October of that year, and after several
attempts to get through to my father on the phone, finally

131

saw him for one of our catch-up dinners. He was full of the death of Wolfe, his writings, his loss to literature, and the whole spectrum of questions and grief that death generates for the remainder at such times. ELM had a simple but adequate phrase to end such discussions; it was this: "It beats the devil." His favorite people, Dreiser, Mencken, Wolfe, Powys, and others were gradually leaving the New York scene. He stated on the way to the Hofbrau at Hoboken one night that life might be "the memory and the influence of that memory of good people." So it went even in the literary capital of the country, a few years prior to the convulsions of the world born in World War II, in the life of Edgar Lee Masters. He was a tolerant philosopher.

Laugh, Lydia, Laugh

I have previously commented on ELM's buffoonery, his delight in playing the clown, of surprising the unsuspecting guest or walking companion with strange comments or antics. This trait of his, boyish and happy, is among my most mirthful memories of him. The well-cultivated portion of this clowning was his love of strange and absurd newspaper ads, particularly the ones covering the miracles of patent medicines and the glorious recovery from illness of many sorts. He would shout with glee when the testimonial carried a picture of the patient, now recovered. He had a perfect foil in this foolishness in the person of H. L. Mencken. They chortled back and forth between Baltimore and New York—kept the mails busy. I have letters and pictures from the fictitious Lute Puckett, Harley Prowler, Elmer Grubb, Dr. Lucious Atherton, and associations with which he amused his selected mailing list. The titles are absurd, but that was the idea; furthermore, the names and declarations of new-found health had the *Spoon River* aroma or flavor. So it came to be that the poem "To An Orphan Clam" is quoted here.

TO AN ORPHAN CLAM

O orphan clam, O orphan clam
You never seem to give a damn,
You ride upon the summer sea
Indifferent as a thing can be.

You do not grieve about your pa,
Nor eke I notice of your ma,
You loll upon the rolling waves,
Without regard to parent's graves.

You do not seem to think at all
Of what you lost, or of the pall
That fell upon you when you lost
Your parents in that holocaust.

When they were boiled and afterward
In sizzling skillets of smoking lard
Were fried to ease the appetite
Of loafers on that fatal night.

You go on careless without thought
For what misfortune thus was wrought
To social state and education
By death's most awful desolation.

No, there you swim along the rollers,
And laugh until you show your molars,
Enjoying winds and waves and sun,
And having thus a lot of fun.

O orphan clam, O orphan clam
I wish to God I was as calm,
I wish that I could sport and laugh
At every lying paragraph.

Thanks for the lesson you have taught,
No matter if it comes to naught.
I'd rather be an orphan clam
Than write the slickest epigram.
                                    —Lute Puckett

This poem is typical of his great interest in Lydia Pinkham's
Vegetable Compound and other remedies that insured health
and sexual vigor. ELM kept a file of these newspaper clip-
pings for his mischievous moods. The corny phrase was not
neglected; he would stop a stranger in a restaurant and say,
"Pardon me, did you know that 'Work Wins' or 'Waste Not

134

Want Not.' " Another favorite was "Little strokes fell great oaks." The results were sometimes beyond his highest expectations—the accosted person's expression was worth the effort. ELM would grab his handkerchief, cover his face, and flee from the eating place, red of face with laughter.

The Tough Letter

It was below zero when I came into our squadron orderly room at the Sioux Falls Army Air Field in 1943 (World War II). On my desk was a letter with familiar typing and the imprint of the Hotel Chelsea. The mail was here despite the snowdrifts and the bad roads.

I sat down to read Father's letter, one of a constant chain that he felt were my due, now that I might be going overseas to fight again for "democracy." This word amused him greatly, and he hated war because he believed wars, the world over, had originated from economic reasons and not to defend democracy.

Nevertheless, this letter was a tough one. He had bitterly despised writing it and I, in turn, was a sad and forlorn reader. It stated, after considerable explanation, that he was in financial difficulties. Esquire had turned down an article he had believed accepted. The Macmillan royalty checks were not sufficient, and he must have money at once.

I was a poor son at this time, trying to live and support my obligations on a captain's pay in the Air Corps. It was a time of low tide for me financially. However, I discussed the matter with my wife, Jean, and we determined to help out as best we could on a regular monthly basis, with a check to the poet as long as needed. Apparently this was a great solace to him, not the insignificant amount toward New York living, but the fact that he received the money regularly each month.

His appreciation made our few sacrifices worthwhile, and, for the record, I must restate that he wrote me the previously quoted letter, telling me that he was leaving me the copyrights to *Spoon River* to compensate for my "generous" action. Perhaps if I had gone to court after his death, the validity of his wish might have been established, but we were all court weary and sick of condemning each other for fancied injustices. I let the royalties and the copyrights go to his wife, Ellen, hoping to put an end to bitterness between my mother and his new wife, as well as endeavoring to pacify my sisters' feeling toward the whole situation. In this thought, perhaps I have been wrong. Maybe my mother's last years would have been happier had I retained and controlled *Spoon River* in the area in which it was created and supported. She never commented about this and I never inquired.

There was this—I saw my mother for the last time for a good visit in 1957. I was in Chicago and had several days with her at her little home in Highland Park. The nurses adored her, and she was comfortable after a period of suffering. We had talked endlessly about everything except my father. She avoided this subject with the consummate skill of an expert conversationalist. I knew she still loved him. The subject of the why's, who's, and what's of the divorce and the suffering incident to it would never be discussed, and yet we both knew that she had but months to live, and duties called me back to Oklahoma. She was propped up in bed. I had given her a glass of wine, holding her head and grieving with her weakness, which seemed a part of me. A radio was going in the next room and she looked at me with that look which said, "My son, I may not talk to you again as we have today." I knew it was our last real visit, with the loving prouncement in her eyes that said, "My only son, I cannot discuss your father anymore."

The fact is, it was our last visit, in the sense of an orderly and quiet conversation. We were never alone again during the short remainder of her lifetime.

Pearl Harbor

On December 7, 1941, Father and I walked into the lobby of his Chelsea Hotel in New York, after a splendid day together. He had indeed covered Menard County and was in a reminiscent mood. The hotel switchboard operator called to us about the tragedy of Pearl Harbor. We had lost a big portion of our U.S. Navy. We could scarcely believe her report at the time, but father's reaction was swift and terrible. "It's war," he remarked. "It will be the rape of Europe and the death of our youth." He was a changed man, thinking immediately of the things he had left to do, in view of the probability of New York's being bombed. My thoughts were on the necessity of getting back to my family in Chicago. Thus we parted for a long time because I was away four years in the U.S. Air Force. He fell on some evil times. The tragedy of it was that his troubles did not reach him until it was too late to prevent them. So the war took much from our togetherness, and at a most critical time in his declining years.

Brother's Wife

We took our customary trip to Central Illinois this year and, as part of the itinerary, stopped in Springfield, Illinois, to visit my cousin Dr. Thomas D. Masters and his wife Mary Jane. We found, during the course of our short stay, that my aunt, Mrs. Thomas D. Masters, Sr., who resides next door to Dr. Tom, was in fine fettle. She wanted to visit, as the saying goes.

I had the fine experience of spending several hours with her. She spent the time relating her many experiences with my father, of whom she was very fond. I say that more important than her affection was her understanding of the man. In addition, she had a collection of his letters that are extraordinary, particularly the ones about his mother and her lack of understanding of his father, Hardin Wallace Masters. Several of them were about his brother, Tom, and his brilliance as a lawyer, at the expense of all else. Many of her comments are best forgotten. To sum up the entire experience, I would stress again two major characteristics of Father's that point up my feelings. He was a most sensitive and lonely man. This was true everwhere I looked. Aunt Gertrude related trips with Father, particularly from Hillsdale, New York, to the west; his gaiety at times, his quotation of poets, his love of the road and the freedom of moving. All of this was very typical of his moods, which changed with the weather. In summary, the visit confirmed my own feelings about Father's traits and his extreme loneliness—aloneness. Consequently, I believe I have avoided a son's emotional reactions and authentically broadened my canvas.

Aunt Gertrude asked me a searching question, "Did I intend to do a real biography of father?" To this, I replied that the term *real* stopped me. I could not conform to the term as she used it. I explained that my position as a son precluded a detached analysis of the man, and in the second place, I did not have the ability to do such a "real" biography. Perhaps, also, in the back of my mind is the aversion to use the raw colors that might be necessary to be "real." My answer amused this wise and old woman and she offered her help, but felt that ELM's letters should be given to her son, Dexter, a competent writer, for his use at a later date. Knowing the Masterses, I agreed to this disposition of his letters.

Too Late

To paint a picture the artist must use different colors to make his shade. In the same manner, one attempting to write, particularly about a parent, must be doubly sure to omit no detail that helps make up the shade of circumstances that so many times lends reality to the things others do that seem incomprehensible.

My two sisters are as different as the two sides of our family, the Jenkinses and the Masterses. One of them seems to have inherited the characteristics of the Jenkinses, while the other has the talent and personality of the Masterses. I love them both, but my younger sister, Marcia, has always been my alter ego.

My mother lived with Marcia for many years. She preferred being with her than with my other sister, Lamb, or with us. This was particularly apparent during my absence in World War II and my subsequent residence in Oklahoma. Mother preferred the city of her birth, Chicago—the city of her triumphs and sorrows and, above all, the city of her friends.

It was quite natural, but equally disastrous, that her will appointed my older sister, Lamb, as executrix. I use *disastrous* in the sense of preserving material and lending understanding to the records that Father left in our home on Kenwood Avenue in Chicago. Not only were many of his books sold to indifferent dealers, but many papers probably disappeared that would have been most valuable to any competent biographer who might attempt an evaluation of

141

Edgar Lee Masters after the generation of sensitive relatives had passed on. Then, perhaps a good biography can be written. I hope so.

In any event, it has been almost twenty years since my mother died, November 26, 1958, and it was just a few weeks ago that I persuaded my sisters to get Mother's papers and records distributed. Even so, it was too late in one instance. I am told that the letters that Tennessee Mitchell (later wife of Sherwood Anderson) had written my father in the late 1920s had been lost, as well as some letters containing observations of Father's on "money."

Tennessee Mitchell was one of my father's loves over the years and, although the letters may have been as tragic as those from any woman desperately in love, as this type so often are, at the same time they were part of the color of the man and should have been preserved. It is the type of loss on which lawsuits are built except, in this instance, the executrix was a relative. She knew, despite my effort to have the entire story preserved, that I could not blame her for missing material even though I had an interest as an heir. Such losses make factual biography difficult to write. Nevertheless, the motive of the person or persons that lost or destroyed the material has my most sympathetic understanding.

Universe Is God

In mind today are the many conversations I had with ELM on religion. He deeply admired the sincere Christian, but he loathed the man who went to church to be seen or because his banker also attended. He was dedicated to a type of pantheistic religion that he first knew as a youth on his grandfather's farm. Unfortunately, he never seemed to find the man or the minister that represented such faith.

It used to amaze me to find him reading the Bible, for his reading ran the gamut of mental experience. I look back on his shelves, for example, and see the following: *The Comedies of Aristophanes* and *Appreciations with an Essay of Style* by Walter Pater. He typically ranged wide as a reader, but the Bible was a constant source of beauty to him. He regarded it as the greatest story ever told, and for pure simple expression to have no equal.

It must be added that he was an admirer of the Koran and *Bhagavad-Gita* as well, and spent many hours in comparative reading and analysis of different religions and their basic doctrines.

You must imagine my astonishment and resentment when my Presbyterian minister in Deerfield, Illinois, who had come to comfort me when father died on March 6, 1950, made the comment that it was too bad he was an atheist. To which I replied that in my heart he had not even been an agnostic but, if a lover of nature and the beautiful, whether it be music, art, or poetry was in fact an atheist, then he was one.

Isn't it strange that we don't take better care of our immortals? A business contract is perpetuated indefinitely by the best legal brains, but the contracts and the beliefs of our poets, painters, and scientists usually are forgotten. How simple to have a reporter ask Father about his religious beliefs in my presence and have his reply preserved. But no, this is not done, or rarely done, on this base of all life or on any less important subject—not done, despite the fact that we knew Father would be among the immortal writers of his age as far back as 1915—nothing done to preserve the intellectual fervor that produced so many moments of sunshine and rain.

Lincoln's New Salem

Some critics, in quest of historical accuracy, believe that ELM created his poem "Anne Rutledge" out of fancy. This is perhaps partially true, although I have never heard any of the Masterses express themselves on the authenticity of Lincoln's attachment for the girl who lived in New Salem. The fact is that the poem stands for itself and needs no defense as written by the poet.

On one of my periodic trips to Petersburg with father, he touched on the claim that the town had on his affections and stated that he might like to return to Petersburg and spend his sunset years. He rambled on about the wealth of story and sentiment that the little village of 2,300 people had for him—the John Armstrong and Anne Rutledge flavor, which the wind running in the grass spelled out in his old dreams. It seemed so strange to me at the time, such an extreme contrast to life's daily path to eternity that I'll always remember his nostalgic remark. I place in general observation that all men have their Anne Rutledges and that the fair lady, created by father for Lincoln, was not the myth that some believe. Furthermore, my Grandfather Masters, who threatened to write a book on William H. Herndon (see the reproduction of his letter), told me that Herndon not only believed that Anne was the tragedy of Lincoln's emotional life, but that he had papers to prove it. As to his own belief, he never expressed himself in my

145

presence. He had too fine a legal mind to accept what he heard as fact.

Suffice it to say, one can stand today at the foot of Anne Rutledge's grave in the lovely little Oakland Cemetery in Petersburg, Illinois, and see Anne and Abe walking hand in hand toward the hills of their youth. You know that Lincoln loved her very much. ELM knew this too. How well he knew it. So it is, I believe, the Anne Rutledge story in all its pathos and charm. I suspect that my father believed it. He believed it to the point of returning to Illinois as an old man to relive his belief. His small room at the Chelsea Hotel in New York, some of his sophisticated and cynical city friends, his love of the lonely city, his occasional drink of rye whiskey before breakfast, not even the overpowering contrast of all of them could still the heartbeat for his clapboard house on the hill in Petersburg, Illinois, the Lincoln country of his youth.

But, of course, he never returned to the house in Petersburg to spend his declining years with the few Masterses who were left. Instead he grew increasingly fearful of crossing Fifth Avenue in New York and finally ended up remaining in the square block of his residence so that he had no street crossings. His crossings became the responsibilities of his younger friends and those members of his family who knew and forgave him the idiosyncrasies that made his pencil move into the centuries. A century from now, let it not be said that the poem "Anne Rutledge" did not represent the bitter failure of a portion of the president's life— nor the poet's story of the failure. How many of us have our failures preserved in such broad colors?

Herndon, a well-known lawyer of his day, was a friend and partner of my grandfather Masters. He wrote and published what is commonly known as Herndon's *Life of Lincoln*. It is a fascinating book, and in it he states: "The

146

courtship with Anne Rutledge and her untimely death form the saddest page in Mr. Lincoln's history. I am aware that most of his biographers have taken issue with me on this phase of Mr. Lincoln's life." I have not mentioned Herndon as a defense of father's poem but as, perhaps, a seldom-mentioned book that should be of interest in connection with the poem.

No Boredom

Five years ago Ellen and Hilary and most of the original remaining Masters clan exchanged letters, at least Christmas greetings. Now there is the silence of indifference. It is just within the last several years that I have finally obtained recognition of the Masters spirit of pride and courage from my two sisters. They are now aware of the tradition of the clan and the splendid people of our family who reside in the Springfield area. I refer specifically to Dr. Tom Masters and his wonderful wife, Mary Jane, and his mother, Gertrude Mettler, who over the years have been such a source of pride and comfort to me. Brilliant and exotic Masterses—sad and gay Masterses—talented and spendthrift Masterses. As my Aunt Gertrude once said, "Any woman who marries a Masters will never die of boredom."

Idiot's Laugh

I have touched before on the friends and acquaintances of Father, who have contacted me through the years after he went to New York. Ironically enough, or perhaps it's just routine, many distinguished Chicagoans have called me to inquire about his health, new writings, and news of him. Some are men I never heard him speak of when he lived in Chicago.

One of these distinguished gentlemen was Carter Harrison, formerly mayor of the city but not one of father's intimates. His call was typical of others received—when I was often at a loss as to how much or what to say. What degree of interest and intimacy did the unknown caller have? I never knew exactly, but the calls and inquiries always evoked a chain of reminiscences. They would each say that they had admired him or had fun with him over the years and perhaps relate how beer mugs were slid down the old Palmer House Bar. This feat was in the days when there were silver dollars imbedded in the bar room floor, and there was no charge for roast beef.

Now all of this made pretty good sense because I remembered the Palmer House Bar in the days when father had his law office at the Ashland Block, a red brick skyscraper of the time, at the corner of Clark and Randolph Streets. This office, I know, was the most fun of all of his Loop offices. It was here he posed as Webster Ford; and here that his imagination ran riot with legal techniques and interpretations of the law.

149

It is not difficult to relive these days of the man from Spoon River. He had come from the grim environs of a small, Central Illinois town with his sheepskin, to practice law. He had studied the statutes alone, with the grim determination to succeed, which personified his whole life; he was going to be a good lawyer in the big city, come hell or high water. He attained his goal. Here is another curious enigma of the man—his ability, through work and dogged determination, to achieve all of his material and business projects, and withal, his tragic failure in many of his spiritual endeavors. I have always felt that this failure to touch the stars that he raced toward all his life in his reading, his emotional capacities, and his inability to find warm companions, was the reason for his great cynicism and bitterness. The world was not his oyster. Many time it seemed a great void of contradictions to him, an amusing spectacle in which he heard the idiots laugh. The baseness of human nature often evoked a terrifying mood in the man. This I have seen, time and time again, in his life. A beautiful morning would turn into a violent, destructive emotional storm. At such times we all got out of the way because his scalpel was too sharp to be borne.

The Will

There is a curious heritage in the Masterses, like sap running in root sprouts from an old tree. It comes to mind when the finality of death comes into the scan of the remaining members. In 1958 I lost my mother, a woman of wondrous courage and charm. She had the resistance of nonresistance and the fierce loyalty of her children, particularly those of her own sex. Her will was an astounding document because it seemed to me to regenerate the troubles and misunderstandings of my father's life.

In the will she appointed my two sisters as co-executrices, to distribute equally her few personal possessions. Already the fruits of this foolishness are ripening. Letters of national interest, perhaps, that belonged to my father, autographed books, and other items of this nature have been buried in the fog of self-protection of the heirs. With the cheerfulness of possession, my older sister has given me five letters of little significance, some silver, three copies of the play *The Leaves of the Tree* (Chicago: The Rook's Press, 1909), and an album of my own photographs taken in 1913. As to going through a mass of material that has been hiding for years, no plan has been made, nor will it be during my lifetime.

Thus the loom spins on as it did when my father fought bitterly with his sister, Madeline Masters Stone, over strangely similar personal belongings of his father. These

151

are the seeds of bitterness that continue to plague the family from generation to generation. The pattern seems so alike to me that it is almost terrifying to be tolerant and reasonable for those of us living in this generation.

An experience with a beloved sister in June of this year brought to mind the many times my father grieved over such things. In the Chicago Loop stands an old building, 127 North Dearborn Street. It was here that my father fled to share an office with a friend, Bill Slack, during his struggle to obtain a divorce and get to New York. There was the fever of unwritten books in his blood. He had been fed the heady wine of a famous man of letters. Each book since *Spoon River* engendered a new urge to get on, to create another masterpiece. He was not thinking nor was he aware of the disaster to fall upon him for the desertion of his family and collateral obligations.

Fateful Pattern

In May of 1941 I was commissioned a captain in the Army
Air Force of the United States and ordered to active duty.
Thus began an absence from Chicago of more than four
years. During this time many critical things began to happen
to Edgar Lee Masters. The passage of the years on people
in middle life seems to first become a problem in two areas,
health and money. Although it is a characteristic of the
Masters clan to think themselves immortal, it is an expensive
theory. My father was no exception to the toll of time.

To go back a bit to gain perspective, when he left Chicago
to reside in New York his divorce had been granted. The
court had made the usual property provisions for my mother
and two sisters. This became an item of contention among
all concerned. So it came to be that when father requested
that certain personal papers, letters, memoranda, and selected books be sent to him in New York, my mother refused
the request, pending payment of back alimony. This action,
of course, be it good or bad, was the source of much bitterness between them. It also colored the thinking of my two
younger sisters, both of them beloved of their father. The
material valuable to the biographer and to the history of
poetry was stored in his trunk at our old family home in
Chicago. My mother kept it under lock and key. It was with
the passage of time forgotten, although I must say that I
was sympathetic to my father's request for its return and,
in fact, did my best to keep his library together. A few of
his books, a very few, I have today, but the majority were

153

sold to the book dealers for a song when our old home was sold in 1942.

As to the personal papers, some of them were moved to the basement of my eldest sister's home. At least, when I returned from World War II, the house was gone, and the contents sold or distributed to other members of the immediate family. The sale of the large old house was a financial move of which I approved at the time. However, the disposition of the valuable papers in this manner has always been a source of deep sorrow to me and a matter I resented very much. It was particularly a blow because, as a young broker, I had been contributing to the family support of both my mother and my two sisters. One of them did not know it at the time, but I had paid her tuition at the University of Chicago and had given her a wedding party. I felt entitled to be consulted; I have always grieved at my inability to return to my father the few personal possessions that he put so much store by before he died.

Thus the Spoon River wheel turns today. It is never ending in its demands on the survivors. Under the terms of my mother's will, the three of us, my two sisters and I, were to share her few personal things, share and share alike. There is no inventory of Father's letters or memos and scant mention made of them in the will. For the record, I have acknowledged receipt of five letters and three books, adding them to my lifelong collection. The letters, marked "notable," are the typical wife-of-a-famous-husband type of correspondence and two letters written by my father concerning my service in the United States Naval Reserve during World War I. The curious Masters history spins on— always it seems to be spinning a senseless and stupid pattern among the children of the poet.

Perhaps it is fortunate that it may end with my generation because there are no children for me. Perhaps the Jenkins-Masters brew was too strong and it may be just as well.

154

What Price Immortality?

I have often reflected on the cost of great books—in lives, in unhappiness, in ancestors, and in progeny. In my father's case, the cost of *Spoon River* had become an astronomical figure by the time my mother died.

The loss of friends over the years is an intangible cost, but, from my own observation, I can think of relatively few old-time friends who remained with father to the last. Quite the contrary, most of the group had been alienated, not to say bitter. Let me review the ones I knew. To begin with, the law partners were all in the unfriendly category: Darrow, Wilson, Slack, and George Jenkins. In a correlative way, an intimate friend of Father's who lived in our home during his own travail, Sam Morgan, was not only unfriendly to my father but went out of his way to support my mother. All of the immediate relatives were indifferent to my father's troubles.

In the winter of 1944-45, Father was living in Charlotte, North Carolina, with his wife, Ellen, and their son, Hilary. I was in the Air Force and just assigned to contract termination work in Raleigh, North Carolina, which made frequent trips to Charlotte over the weekend a wonderful occasion. So it was that we had many visits in his small hotel room. It was during this time that I became so aware of his bitterness and his loneliness in relation to old friends and to relatives. Father would start many conversations with the query, "My boy, what has happened to so-and-so?" Many times he would go into an era I did not know. When I answered and brought him up-to-date on the individual, he would often make the familiar hissing sound accompanied by a bitter or scurrilous comment on the individual. The hissing sound was indeed a prominent characteristic of my father. He made it with a petulant and scornful lip, and both the sound that emitted and his expression were perfect in their contempt. The point being that it was obvious that many people who had been fond of him had been driven to indifference or worse because of his divorce from my mother or his inability to overlook the faults of others. He had a vitriolic and bitter tongue, as his mother before him, and it took a heart-rending toll over the years.

Finally, when the end came to a great American poet, the services were attended by a modest roomful of people, perhaps not more than fifty. A few came from Chicago, a few from Petersburg, and a few from New York. The services were held in an old home in Petersburg that held boyhood memories for my father. It was a severe service, with the music of Beethoven, which he loved, and brought back memories to me of his little, bare room at the Chelsea Hotel. It was a forlorn and hopeless service, but in a way, I guess, he had requested it.

Last summer my wife and I stopped again at the little cemetery in Petersburg where Father and the Masterses are all buried. It was sunny, peaceful, and full of that historic atmosphere of the Lincoln country that he loved as a boy, riding the hills of his grandfather's farm. He was at peace. The old oak trees told me so. The price was paid.

Best Poems

Again we were talking about Father's best poems.

The gray-toned catalpa in the back yard didn't seem to care. The view from the sparsely furnished living room in the Chelsea that father used as a writing room had not improved any since my last visit.

The room, however, was quiet except for an occasional slam of the iron-grilled elevator door. My father had enjoyed some seventy years of wonderful health, but his mind had arrived at the point of going back to his youth in Chicago, his boyhood in Petersburg, and, of course, his prolific works since 1925. Much of the reminiscence took place in the room in which we were sitting. Many poems were born there and much poetry discussed with New York's literary people.

Now again, the oft-repeated question, "My boy, what do you think is my best poem in *Toward the Gulf?*"

My love of parent exceeded my knowledge of literature, particularly poetry, and I tried to answer in my layman's fashion. This always evoked long explanations of the errors in my choice and my obtuse perception.

However, many positive things happened. One day, a Sunday afternoon, Father said, I'll tell you my best poems and don't you forget it." So saying, he took my copy of *Selected Poems* and marked his selections. Here they are, as marked on this occasion:

The Corn
St. Francis and Lady
  Clare
Gabriel and Zacharias
Judas Iscariot
The Hittites

Tulips
In the Garden
Branch Mollusca
Lithographs and Life
Love and Beauty
Golden Gate Park

New York
Worlds
The Hill
Lucinda Matlock
Fiddler Jones
Immanuel Reedy

Readers choice (either of the
  following could have been
  selected because the mark
  is marginal) :
The Statue
My Light With Yours

Her Favorite Poems

It has been said that chance plays strange tricks upon us. It does.

I had been talking to a fascinating lady. She said, "So you are Edgar Lee Masters's son?" This question developed into one of those unusual, interesting discussions that sometimes make casual introductions and cocktail parties worthwhile.

She recounted her affection for my father, his peculiar type of genius, times in Brown County, Indiana, and her many talks with him about his poems. She was a tactful and discerning lady. I was very, very interested in this chance meeting.

I rushed home at the time and made the following notes, among other notations, of this meeting.

She had commented that *Spoon River Anthology* was not Father's best book in her opinion, but it was the most interesting. Her favorite poems were: "William and Emily," "Calvin Campbell," "Hortense Robbins," "Lucinda Matlock," "Anne Rutledge," "Henry Phipps," "Mrs. Merritt," "Alfred Moir," "Searcy Foote," " Roy Butler," "Pauline Barraett," "Julia Miller," and "Deacon Taylor."

Perhaps these poems were in a sense her biography. I feel sure that some of them were autobiographical to my father.

The lovely lady is gone now, but the autumn foliage in Brown County, Indiana, remains an annual triumph of color. The little towns of Elkinsville, Story, and Nashville are an epilogue to an old story.

159

The Portrait

I received a letter from my talented cousin, Dexter Masters, telling me that a New York artist had an oil painting of ELM. He went on to relate that Ivan Oppfer, who had a studio at 10 East Eighth Street in New York City, was considered a fine portrait painter. The portrait of Father had been completed about 1941 and was autographed by father before the canvas had dried.

For the record, I had not heard of any oil painting that had been completed of the man and was tremendously interested in it. All of this resulted in a correspondence back and forth with Oppfer, who also sent me a photograph of the painting. We finally agreed on a price and the painting was shipped to me.

It is a fine oil for me because I have seen Father in the mood depicted here many times over the years. It applied especially well to his days at the Chelsea Hotel in New York where he had sat before me in conversation, looking in the same retrospective way that the painting portrays.

Naturally, I am delighted with this painting that practically speaks, maybe not to others, but most assuredly to me. It has hung in my study for ten years now, and many are the visits I have had with the departed father and poet through the painting. It speaks to me on many occasions—almost every morning.

Recently an old friend from my Chicago days, now transplanted to Oklahoma, retired from business, and he became

This is the portrait of Edgar Lee Masters, painted by Ivan Oppfer of New York City and completed in 1941.

161

interested in painting. As a collateral interest, he took over the guidance and operation of a fine but small art gallery. It has grown rapidly under his practical judgment and care, and when my gallery friend conceived the idea of having an exhibit of paintings owned by friends and members of his art gallery, he suggested I might enter Father's portrait. After inquiring about insurance coverage and other routine items involved in such an exhibit, I agreed to lend the portrait and one landscape to the showing. I removed it from my study wall, wrapped it carefully in heavy paper and put it in the back seat of my car to transport to the museum for the exhibit.

A series of strange incidents then took place. My proud wirehaired terrier, Pepper, a constant companion over the weekend, jumped from the front to the back seat of the automobile and landed on the side of the canvas. I had visions of tears, marks, irreparable damage to the treasured portrait, but no such thing. The protective wrapping plus my anguished shout when he made the leap saved the day; not a blemish on it.

We arrived at the art museum with the picture and registered it with the attendant. It was to be hung by the committee for the show later in the day, and I would see it when I returned to the showing the next day. I started home and was overcome by a feeling of remorse—a strange foreboding of disaster. The portrait would not be hanging in my study when I arrived—I had loaned it to the museum. This was foolhardy to have done. The painting could not be replaced, for both the subject and the artist were gone. Suppose it were stolen? Perhaps a fire would break out in the old museum after the attendant had gone. More compelling than all this was the inner voice, as I drove along, saying, "Go back and get the painting—go back—go back." Finally I could take it no longer. I could not return home

162

without my father's portrait. I turned the car around and went back to the museum. I was just in time, the attendant was closing up. I said to her, "I've returned for my painting. I cannot leave it here. It is out of place in a landscape exhibit." She looked astonished but understanding and said, "Very well, bring us another to replace it tomorrow."

Playwright

These were the days—Vachel Lindsay had written *The Santa Fe Trail*. Jo Davidson, a sculptor friend, was a frequent visitor to father's apartment at the Chelsea. Compatible souls he claimed in understanding and numbers not available in Chicago. In addition, William Lyon Phelps was available for talks and praised some of Father's poems and biographies. They were part of an active group that had rapport and visited back and forth when the spirit tired of writing and painting.

In September of the year we had a long discussion in his small living room at the hotel about his plays. He told me that although it was an abortive effort, he had worked hard on them, inspired and driven by the hope of getting one of them on Broadway and "making some money." The plays were all written in Chicago about 1905 to 1909, and published by the Rooks Press. He was encouraged about them when one of America's great actresses, Minnie Maddern Fiske, had become interested in them, but her producer wouldn't produce. The producer, money man, wanted severe cuts and changes; however, typical of ELM, there were no changes made. For the record, there were four plays written: *The Locket, Althea, The Trifler,* and *The Leaves of the Tree*. The discourse ended that day by the presentation of a leather book containing three of the plays and inscribed, "For my son, Hardin Wallace Masters, with great love."

164

Now the book is, indeed, a proud possession in my library. I have never seen another copy, and the volume is of special significance because the subject of the plays has been forgotten. My cousin, Mary Jane Masters, advised me that her Players Guild in Springfield, Illinois, was putting on some different plays this summer (1973) and regretted ELM had never written any plays.

Just after the turn of the century, ELM wrote and published a play entitled *Maximilian,* about the Archduke of Austria and the years 1866-67. So it is that Father attempted five plays, all well written and better than most we see today, but they never made the stage.

Last Trip

It is a typical gray March morning in Chicago, March 6, 1950, and a telegram from Ellen Masters arrives, telling me of Father's death shortly after midnight. He died in a small nursing home in Melrose Park, Pennsylvania, close to the school where his wife was teaching. The services were set three days later in his boyhood town of Petersburg, Illinois—his heart's home.

It was difficult to realize that he was gone because, actually, he had moved away as my father when he remarried, although I always believed that I had understood his marital life. Beloved people that we do not have daily contact with, in a manner, die a little in our everyday thinking. Occasionally the nourishment is in a phone call, a smile over the horizon of memory, but little impact is really made on our daily road to the same end. Thus I thought, the immortal man is gone from his bed and from the Chelsea Hotel but will always be with me as a father, except that there will be no more letters and no more visits. It is, of course, more than this even, with dozens of books living in one's library to regenerate the man for me.

I checked the trains to Springfield, Illinois, and found father's body would arrive early in the morning on Thursday.

At the appointed time I waited at the Grand Central Station for the arrival of the casket and found that Father was as lonely in death as he had been sometimes in life. I was the only one there when the bored station attendant nodded toward the box standing on the station truck to be wheeled to the Illinois Central train. I walked beside it, down the trackway, as long as possible and finally realized that I could go no further.

Fog, sleet, and smoke swirled around me in the dim station areaway. The small baggage truck and its casket disappeared into the freight room for its last trip across Chicago's streets to the Illinois Central station. Ironically enough, the train to Springfield, Illinois, recalled the memory of happy summer days. This was the station where we had taken the train together to Michigan to visit Hardy Masters.

My grandfather Masters had a farm near Saugatuck, Michigan, in the early twenties, and the way was by Pere Marquette train to Fennville. He bought this small acreage, actually a cherry orchard, at the insistence of ELM. It was on the shores of Lake Michigan with a superb view from the porch of its comfortable house. Here he spent the summers of his sunset years, visited by his immediate family and his grandchildren. I looked forward avidly each year during this era, to my visit to the Masters farm, and I am sure that my father did, too. He was particularly fond of Saugatuck, the wind-curved dunes, the Pines, and above all, the boat trip from Chicago. I can see him now, raising his hand in proud salute to his father as the boat docked. My grandfather, standing on the dock as straight as an Indian brave, with his mane of white hair and penetrating eyes, was waiting to give his humorous greeting to another summer in Michigan. My father worshipped this occasion and would always laugh and say, "Well, well, father," and off we would go to breakfast at the little hotel and much discussion of the law. My grandfather always knew that this was father's favorite time. They got back to Petersburg and to the history that always fascinated him and that produced *Spoon River*. Many of these epitaphs came from his father's stories of his boyhood.

167

Appendix A
Books

A few of the books that belonged to Edgar Lee Masters, now part of my library, show the range of Father's reading and literary interests:

The Best Poems of 1929—Thomas Moult
How to Write a Good Play (undated)—Frank Archer
The Jolly Beggars (1914)—Robert Burns
Walker's Rhyming Dictionary (1902)—J. Walker
The Winning of the West (1889)—Theodore Roosevelt
William the Third (1888)—H. D. Traill
The Romance of Leonardo da Vinci (1902)—Dmitri Merejkowski
Schopenhauer's Essays (undated)—T. Bailey Saunders
Adam Smith's Moral Sentiments (1892)—Dugald Stewart
The Fear of Living (1913)—Henry Bordeaux
Death (1912)—Maurice Maeterlinck
Crime (1922)—Clarence Darrow
Robespierre (1908)—Hilaire Belloc
Native Tales of New Mexico (1932)—Frank Applegate
The Complex Vision (1920)—John Cowper Powys
Sketches, New and Old (1884)—Mark Twain
The Road of Living Men (1913)—Will Levington Comfort
Philosophy of History (1904)—G. F. W. Hegel
Orloff and His Wife (1909)—Maxim Gorky
The Perfect Wagnerite (1909)—Bernard Shaw
The Book of the Dead (1915)—Sir Alfred Wallace Budge
The Marriage of Heaven and Hell (1914)—William Blake
Epictetus (1892)—T. W. Rolleston

168

Plays From Moliere (1889)
Cicero's Orations (1909)
Dictionary of English Synonyms (1914)—Thoms Fenby
Sword Blades and Poppy Seed (1915)—Amy Lowell
William Tell (undated)—Johann Christoph Frederich von Schiller
Byron's Letters (1887)
Appreciations (1902)—Walter Pater
The Greek Anthology (1917)—James Hutton, ed.
The Comedies of Aristophanes (1905)
Suetonius' Lives of the Caesars (1909)—Alexander Thomson, M.D., ed.
The Journal of a Recluse (1909)—from Mary Fisher
The Divine Fire (1904)—May Sinclair
Homo Sapiens (1927)—Byzybyszewski
Tom Jones (1908)—Henry Fielding
North of Boston (1914)—Robert Frost
Pagan and Christian Creeds (1920)—Edward Carpenter
Poems Every Child Should Know (1904)—Mary E. Burt, ed.
The Poems of Corinne Roosevelt Robinson (1921)
Good Morning America (1928)—Carl Sandburg
The Heroes (1911)—Charles Kingsley
The Titan (1914)—Theodore Dreiser
The Life of the Bee (1906)—Maurice Maeterlinck
Down Among Men (1913)—Will Levington Comfort
The Iliad (1908)—A. J. Church, trans.
Rudyard Kipling's Verse (1924)
The Life of Benvenuto Cellini (1905)—John Addington Symonds
Beasts, Men and Gods (1924)—Ossendowski
Dryden's Virgil (1907)
Wuthering Heights (1907)—Emily Brontë
The Book of Elizabethan Verse (1907)
The Best Poems and Essays of Edgar Allan Poe (1903)—Sherwin Cody
Walden (1908)—Henry David Thoreau
The History of Rome (undated)—Theodor Mommsen
Le Morte D'Arthur (1906)—Thomas Malory
The Man Who Married a Dumb Wife (1921)—Anatole France
Sapho (1909)—Alphonse Daudet
History of the Popes (1907)—Leopold Von Ranke
Gulliver's Travels (1910)—Jonathan Swift

A Journal of the Great War (1922)—Charles G. Dawes
An Economic Interpretation of the Constitution of the United States (1926)—Charles Beard
Dead Souls (undated)—Nikolai Vasilievich Gogol
Glouchester Moors (1901)—William Vaughn Moody
Paradise Lost (1855)—John Milton

Appendix B

People

In sketching a life as you saw it, it seems to me that three other lists have bearing on the picture and add perspective to the work. This is a list composed of all the individuals I can recall who had a major or important impact on ELM's life—the day-to-day travel.

Al Austrian
Louis Aehl
Zoe Akins
Judge Frank Blane
William Jennings Bryan
Pearl Buck
Dr. Richard Burke
Dr. George Coleman
Willie Carlin
Clarence Darrow
Jo Davidson
Theodore Dreiser
Charles Gates Dawes
John Dewey
August Derleth
John Gould Fletcher
Percy Grainger
Alice Corbin Henderson
Burton Holmes
Robinson Jeffers
Senator LaFollette
Judge Kenesaw Mountain
  Landis
Vachel Lindsay
Jack London
Amy Lowell

Percy MacKay
Ernest McGaffey
H. L. Mencken
Abe Meyer
Edna St. Vincent Millay
Harriet Monroe
Samuel Morgan
William Lyon Phelps
John Cowper Powys
William Marion Reedy
Edwin Parsons Reese
Edwin Arlington Robinson
Theodore Roosevelt
Carl Sandburg
Charles W. Shippey
Will Shuster
William Slack
John Sloan
Ida M. Tarbell
Sara Teasdale
Dr. Willard Thorp
Eunice Tietgens
Ridgeley Torrence
Francis Wilson
Thomas Wolfe

171

Appendix C
Places

ELM was most sensitive to places or locale, if you will. I reflect on them with a strong brush, having been to all of them with him.

Chicago, Illinois
Lewistown, Illinois
New York, New York
Petersburg, Illinois
Spring Lake, Michigan
Rex Terrace, Michigan
San Francisco, California
Saugatuck, Michigan
St. Louis, Missouri
Tremont, Indiana (the dunes)

Appendix D
Favorite Eating Places
("Feeding Places" Frequented by ELM)

CHICAGO

Cliff Dwellers
Illinois Athletic Club
Berghof
Henrici's
Brevoort
Palmer House

NEW YORK

Players Club
Cavanaughs
Automat
Luchows
Jack Dempseys
Hoboken, N. J., Hoffbrau
Gourmet Society

NOTE: "Feeding place" is a harsh phrase. I use it because the poet enjoyed it. He used it frequently, salted with his inimitable laugh, as a derisive expression, saying, "Just look at those people 'feeding.'"

Bibliography

In addition to the list of books that Edgar Lee Masters owned (Appendix A), for flavor and character I am listing the following because they are an inherent part of the philosophy of this sketchbook.

Comfort, Will Levington. *Midstream*. New York: Doran, 1914.

Corbin, Alice. *Red Earth*. Chicago: Seymour, 1920.

Darrow, Clarence. *The Plea of Clarence Darrow*. Chicago: Seymour, 1924.

———. *The Story of My Life*. New York: Scribner, 1932.

Dreiser, Theodore. *Sister Carrie*. New York: Boni and Liveright, 1917.

Drury, John. *Old Illinois Houses*. Springfield, Ill.: Illinois State Historical Society, 1948.

Frost, Robert. *North of Boston*. New York: Henry Holt, 1914.

Henderson, Alice Corbin. *Brothers of Light*. New York: Harcourt Brace, 1937.

Herndon, William H. *Life of Lincoln*. New York: World Publishing Co., 1965.

Jeffers, Robinson. *Selected Poetry*. New York: Random House, 1938.

Jenkins, Robert E. *Jenkins Family Book*. Chicago: Privately published, 1904.

Kramer, Dale. *Chicago Renaissance*. New York: Appleton, 1966.

London, Charmain. *The Book of Jack London*. New York: Century, 1921.

Powys, John Cowper. *The Complex Vision*. New York: Dodd, Mead, 1920.

Sandburg, Carl. *Abraham Lincoln, The Prairie Years*. New York: Harcourt Brace, 1954.

Seymour, Ralph Fletcher. *Some Went This Way*. Chicago: Seymour, 1945.

Mark Twain's Autobiography. New York: Harper, 1924.

Wagengnecht, Edward. *Chicago*. Norman, Okla.: University of Oklahoma Press, 1964.

BOOKS BY EDGAR LEE MASTERS

A Book of Verses. Chicago: Way & Williams, 1898.

Maximillian. Boston: The Gorham Press, 1902.

The New Star Chamber and Other Essays. Chicago: Hammersmark Publishing Company, 1904.

The Blood of the Prophets. Chicago: The Rooks Press, 1905.

Althea. Chicago: The Rooks Press, 1907.

The Trifler. Chicago: The Rooks Press, 1908.

The Leaves of the Tree. Chicago: The Rooks Press, 1909.

The Locket. Chicago: The Rooks Press, 1910.

Songs and Sonnets. Chicago: The Rooks Press, 1910.

Spoon River Anthology. New York: Macmillan, 1915.

Songs and Satires. New York: Macmillan, 1916.

The Great Valley. New York: Macmillan, 1916.

Toward the Gulf. New York: Macmillan, 1918.

Starved Rock. New York: Macmillan, 1919.

Mitch Miller. New York: Grosset & Dunlap, 1920.

Domesday Book. New York: Macmillan, 1920.

The Open Sea. New York: Macmillan, 1921.

Children of the Market Place. New York: Macmillan, 1922.

Skeeters Kirby. New York: Macmillan, 1923.

The Nuptial Flight. New York: Boni & Liveright, 1923.

Mirage. New York: Boni & Liveright, 1924.

The New Spoon River. New York: Macmillan, 1924.

Selected Poems. New York: Macmillan, 1925.

Lee, A Dramatic Poem. New York: Macmillan, 1926.

Kit O'Brien. New York: Boni & Liveright, 1927.

Levy Mayer. New Haven, Conn.: Yale University Press, 1927.

Jack Kelso. New York: D. Appleton, 1928.

175

The Fate of the Jury. New York: D. Appleton, 1929.

Gettysburg, Manilla, Acoma. New York: Horace Liveright, 1930.

Lichee Nuts. New York: Horace Liveright, 1930.

Lincoln—The Man. New York: Dodd, Mead, 1931.

Godbey. New York: Dodd, Mead, 1931.

The Serpent in the Wilderness. New York: Sheldon Dick, 1933.

The Tale of Chicago. New York: G. P. Putnam's Sons, 1933.

Dramatic Duologues. London: Samuel French, 1934.

Richmond. London: Samuel French, 1934.

Invisible Landscapes. New York: Macmillan, 1935.

Vachel Lindsay. New York: Charles Scribner, 1935.

Across Spoon River. New York: Farrar & Rinehart, 1936.

The Golden Fleece of California. Weston, Vt.: Countryman Press, 1936.

The New World. New York: D. Appleton-Century, 1937.

Whitman. New York: Charles Scribner's Sons, 1937.

The Tide of Time. New York: Farrar & Rinehart, 1937.

Mark Twain. New York: Charles Scribner's Sons, 1938.

Poems of People. New York: D. Appleton-Century, 1939.

More People. New York: D. Appleton-Century, 1939.

Emerson. New York: Longmans, Green, 1940.

Illinois Poems. Prairie City, Ill.: James A. Decker, 1941.

The Sangamon. New York: Farrar & Rinehart, 1942.

NOTE: The number and variety of books written by ELM will surprise many readers: poetry, particularly fiction, plays, and biographies being among the above titles. Some of these books were presented to Knox College by me, others are in my library. (Knox College has one of the finest and most complete collections of Father's books.)

Index

Johns Hopkins Hospital 131
Journal of the Great Wars, A 39
"Judas Iscariot" 158
"Julia Miller" 159

Kaduker 62
Keats, John 13
Kentucky Derby 94
Kenwood Avenue 33, 34, 35, 50, 56, 64, 71, 76, 78, 103, 141
Kenwood Evangelical Church 36
Knox College (Academy) 13, 23
Kreymborg, Alfred 12

La Collina 11
La Follette 11
Lake Michigan 27, 107, 167
Lake Shore Drive 27
Landis, Judge Kenesaw Mountain 43, 83
La Scala 11
Leaves of the Tree, The 151, 164
Lewiston, Illinois 73, 75, 124, 126
Life of Lincoln 146
Lincoln, Abraham 32, 98, 101, 124, 145, 146, 147, 156
Lindsay, Vachel 11, 35, 83, 131, 164
"Lithographs and Light" 158
Locket, The 164
"Love and Beauty" 158
Lowell, Amy 55, 59
Lower Alton 29
Luchow's Restaurant 131
"Lincinda Matlock" 127, 158, 159
Lydia Pinkham's Vegetable Compound 134

Macmillan 61, 76, 84, 121, 136
Maeterlinck, Maurice 109
Maine 102
Manitou 27
Manodnock Building 113
Maples, The 36
Mark Twain 62, 84
Marquette Building 66, 67, 113
Masefield, John 42
Mason County 21

Masters, Dexter 121, 140, 160
Masters, Edgar Lee 11–3, 15–7, 21–3, 30, 32, 36, 38, 39, 42, 43, 46, 47, 49, 52–5, 58–61, 65, 66, 68–70, 73, 79, 80, 82, 84–7, 89, 90, 96, 101, 103, 105, 106, 108, 112, 114–21, 126, 129–35, 140, 142, 143, 145, 146, 153, 159–61, 164, 165
Masters, Ellen Coyne 81, 88, 117, 121, 122, 137, 148, 155, 166
Masters, Emma Jerusha (Dexter) 21, 106
Masters, Gertrude 139, 140, 148
Masters, Hardin Wallace 13, 16, 35, 48, 58, 61, 62, 65, 67, 71, 75, 91, 93–7, 102, 106, 139, 164
Masters, Hardy 23, 40, 101, 167
Masters, Helen 68, 106
Masters, Hilary 122, 148, 155
Masters, Jean 136
Masters, Lamb 141
Masters, Lucinda (Wasson) 30, 31, 37, 73, 95, 106, 126
Masters, Madeline (Stone) 57, 70, 106, 151
Masters, Marcia, 33, 42, 56, 57, 141
Masters, Mary Jane (Mrs. Thomas D.) 139, 148, 165
Masters Memorial Home 29
Masters, Squire Davis 24, 28, 30, 31, 34, 37, 73, 95, 106, 126
Masters, Dr. Thomas D. 94, 95, 117, 139, 148
Masters, Wilbur 24, 73, 126
Maximilian 120, 165
Mayer, Meyer, Austrian & Platt 43
McCormick, Colonel Robert 114
Melrose Park, Pennsylvania 46, 166
Menard County 37, 84, 97, 126, 127, 138
Mencken, Henry L. 55, 120, 121, 130, 133
Meyer, Abraham 43, 83
Michigan 26, 27, 40, 53, 65, 73, 107, 128, 167
Michigan Avenue 38
Michigan Boulevard 102, 112

179

180

181